Materials & Methods for HISTORY RESEARCH

Library Edition

By Carla Stoffle & Simon Karter

A Division Of Neal·Schuman Publishers, Inc.

Published by The Libraryworks
A Division of Neal-Schuman Publishers, Inc.
64 University Place, New York, N.Y. 10003
Copyright © 1979 by Neal-Schuman Publishers, Inc.

79-306

Library of Congress Cataloging in Publication Data
Stoffle, Carla J.
  Materials & methods for history research.
  (Bibliographic instruction series)
  Bibliography: p.
  1. Historical research—Handbooks, manuals,
etc. 2. History—Methodology—Handbooks, manuals,
etc. I. Dobyns, Henry F., joint author. II. Ti-
tle. III. Series.
D13.S84   907'.2   79-306
ISBN 0-918212-07-3
ISBN 0-918212-06-5 pbk.

Contents

Preface

Materials & Methods for History Research is the first publication of the "Materials & Methods" bibliographic instruction series developed by Carla Stoffle, Associate Director, Library/Learning Center, and Assistant to the Chancellor, University of Wisconsin, Parkside, and Henry F. Dobyns, Visiting Professor of Anthropology, University of Florida at Gainesville. Basic to the series is the discipline-oriented workbook, developed and tested in the classroom by librarians and teaching faculty. Intended to guide students through the maze of information sources encountered during their studies, the workbooks are based on the principle that the more students know about the materials and methods required for effective information gathering in their subject discipline, the more productive they will become.

This library edition of *Materials & Methods for History Research* is comprised of the workbook and an instructor's manual. The workbook introduces students to—and requires them to use—a wide variety of reference tools. Chapter by chapter, guides, subject dictionaries, encyclopedias, biographical sources, indexes, abstracts, bibliographies, periodicals, and government documents are explored. The instructor's manual offers suggestions to librarians and teachers; explains the features of the workbook; provides grading, assignment, and scheduling instructions; and includes individualized fill-ins and answers for the problems and questions found in the workbook.

Both the instructor's manual and the workbook are available separately, designed for course adoption. This one-volume, hard cover edition has been published to serve as a reference tool in and of itself, as well as a text for staff training in bibliographic instruction.

Materials & Methods
for
History Research
Instructor's Manual

Table of Contents

Preface

Materials & Methods for History Research is designed to familiarize history students with the basic types of information sources available in the discipline, to introduce important examples of each type, and to prepare students to use those information sources efficiently and effectively. The workbook consists of brief textual discussions of individual types of sources, and assignments requiring students to use important examples of each type. Instruction and immediate practical application are thus blended to maximize student learning.

The workbook is modeled on the lab manuals used in many science courses. This format was selected after examination of, and experimentation with, several alternative methods for teaching library research skills. There are several advantages in teaching these skills in this manner: (1) the content is broken down into small units that can be mastered easily; (2) the exercises immediately reinforce the textual and class presentation of information; (3) the students actively participate in the learning process; (4) students receive immediate feedback about their progress; (5) student confusion or failure to master the skills can be easily and immediately detected; (6) additional instruction can be provided for those who need it while those who do not can proceed at their own pace; and (7) the number of students that can be taught simultaneously can vary significantly, and almost any course setting, from a separate course to a module within a course, can be used.

As well as introducing principal types of information sources, and principal examples of each type, the workbook is designed to provide students an opportunity to use the sources in a systematic way. It discusses research strategies and the mechanics of the research process, and requires, in the last assignment, that students undertake a research project utilizing the previously learned sources and skills.

The development of the workbook was funded in part by a Teaching Improvement Grant from the University of Wisconsin System, and is the product of four years of experimentation by librarians and historians at the University of Wisconsin-Parkside. During the first year, the instructors relied upon lectures to familiarize students with categories of information sources based on those discussed in Carl White's *Sources of Information in the Social Sciences* (Chicago: American Library Association, 1973), Helen Poulton's *Historian's Handbook* (Norman: University of Oklahoma Press, 1972), Thelma Freides' *Literature and Bibliography of the Social Sciences* (New York: Wiley, 1973), and Jean Gates' *Guide to the Use of Books and Libraries* (New York: McGraw-Hill, 1973). In subsequent years, the categories were refined and the lectures were distilled to form these brief learning workbook chapters with clearly stated objectives and assignments that require students to use the sources annotated in each chapter.

This Instructor's Manual is divided into eight sections. Section I describes the organization and scope of the workbook, and identifies its objectives. A description of how best to use the workbook is provided in Section II, as well as suggestions for its use in settings other than a three credit course. Specific suggestions regarding instructional procedures, the role of the library staff, and sources used are given in Section III. An itemized checklist comprises Section IV, identifying nine tasks for the instructor to accomplish. Section V provides sample instructions to guide the faculty member in preparing instructions to the students for the course. A Checklist of Titles Used, in Section VI, enables the instructor to determine whether the library owns the exact editions of titles used for the assignments. And Sections VII and VIII are included to save the instructor the time consuming chore of creating and testing individual question sets for use with the workbook.

1
Arrangement and Scope of the Workbook

The specific objectives of the workbook are to teach students:

1) to identify and use specialized historical reference sources such as guides, subject dictionaries and encyclopedias, biographical sources, indexes, abstracts, and bibliographies;
2) to locate articles and book reviews in historical journals;
3) to locate and use newspaper articles in research;
4) to locate and use government publications in research;
5) to evaluate the quality of books by using reviews and other criteria discussed in the workbook;
6) to utilize specific research techniques and search strategies for efficient and effective information gathering; and
7) to cite periodicals, books, and documents according to standard bibliographic form.

The workbook is organized into thirteen chapters. Each of the first twelve describes the purposes and utility of one category or type of publication. Examples of each type are annotated. The sources used as examples were selected after a review of historical bibliographies and guides, and on the basis of three criteria: they are all in the English language; they are generally available in medium sized college libraries; they are important examples of the types of sources most useful to history majors.

The assignments accompanying each chapter insure that students immediately use the sources and techniques discussed. The questions pose specific study or research problems. Since needless frustration can only hinder learning, there are no "trick," or even very difficult questions. Each question is phrased in a manner that reiterates points made in the text about the general utility of a type of source and/or the special utility of an individual source.

To introduce students to sources that list reference works, the first chapter focuses on guides to the literature. Chapters Two through Six introduce content reference sources: handbooks, yearbooks and almanacs, atlases, subject dictionaries and encyclopedias, and biographical dictionaries. Chapters Seven and Eight introduce the principal types of finding aids: indexes, abstracts, and bibliographies.

The focus of the workbook then shifts away from reference materials. In Chapter Nine, scholarly journals are discussed; in Chapter Ten, methods for evaluating the quality of monographs are suggested. Chapters Eleven and Twelve focus on two types of "primary" source material, newspapers and government publications, and upon the finding aids available for their efficient use. Chapter Thirteen, the last chapter, consists of a discussion of strategies, mechanics, and methods for efficient library research. Students are asked to define a research topic and prepare a bibliography, using as many of the types of sources introduced in the previous chapters as may be appropriate. This summary assignment requires students to review the preceding chapters. It reiterates for them the interrelated utility of the sources discussed in the separate chapters, and demonstrates to them that in a relatively short time they have learned much about the library's resources and how to use them.

On the average, the workbook absorbs roughly 25 hours of out-of-class student time. Individual assignment sheet questions should require no more than 20 minutes, although at first they often require more time since students are generally unfamiliar with reference sources.

2
Use of the Workbook

At the University of Wisconsin-Parkside, the workbook is used as an integral part of a three credit history methods course. A librarian teaches the four weeks of the course that focus on library research. The class meets in the library, thereby creating a lab environment where students must locate and use specified publications to complete their assignments. With the exception of periodicals, which must be kept on reserve for the duration to insure their availability, all of the noncirculating publications used in the assignments are left in their normal place in the library. A comfortable familiarity with the reference area is one of the benefits students derive from using the workbook.

At the introductory meeting, the librarian describes the workbook, its purposes and organization, and the procedures that will be followed. Students who have had no previous library instruction are given a tour of the library and are offered supplementary instruction on the card catalogue. Attendance at subsequent class sessions is optional, although most students do attend. At these sessions the librarian provides additional information about the uses and organization of the types of sources discussed in the assigned chapters, and answers questions. Students are expected to have read the appropriate chapters and completed the assignments before each class period.

To discourage self-defeating forms of student co-operation, the assignments are individualized. Although every student reads the same question, each is asked for a different item of information. Each question contains a "fill-in" space or spaces designated by the black underlines. Twenty different sets of fill-ins—containing the specific information requests—are provided in Section VII. Copies of these fill-in sheets are distributed to the students along with instruction sheets (see Section V). When more than twenty students are enrolled in the course, some sets of fill-ins are given to more than one student. Each student is asked to transfer the "fill-in" information from the sheet to the workbook.

Assignments may be turned in during the class period or may be placed in a specially marked container next to the reference desk in the library. Assignments are corrected daily by the librarian (using the answer sheets in Section VIII), and are placed on des-ignated shelves in the reference area so that students may pick them up and continue their work without delay. Credit is not given for a chapter until all questions are answered correctly. When students must make a correction, they are instructed to ask the reference librarian on duty for help. The reference librarian thus becomes a tutor, providing the student with whatever instruction is necessary to correct the mistake. And, the student becomes familiar not only with the library's resources, but also with its personnel and their willingness to assist students.

The workbook is graded on a pass-fail basis. No credit is given until all the questions in all the assignments are correctly answered. In addition, the bibliography assigned in Chapter Thirteen must be completed to the satisfaction of both the librarian and the faculty member in charge of the course. The specific criteria used in grading the bibliography at the University of Wisconsin-Parkside are included with the instructions handed out to the students when they begin the workbook (see Section V). The history faculty member in charge of the course gives students who do not complete the work satisfactorily a grade of incomplete for the course, or a failing grade for that portion of the course.

The workbook can effectively be used in settings other than a three credit methods course. These include: other history courses with a research focus; one or two credit courses devoted exclusively to historical bibliography; independent or guided study courses; noncredit study or continuing education programs; and graduate library science courses. In credit history courses, faculty may wish to employ team teaching techniques similar to those used at the University of Wisconsin-Parkside.

Faculty who wish to use the workbook but who do not want to devote a significant amount of class time to it or who wish to have students use the workbook independently, should contact the library staff for support services and suggestions. Arrangements might be made for students to rely upon specified library staff members for tutorial assistance while they are completing the assignments. It may be possible to have the library staff distribute the fill-in sheets and grade the assignments as well.

For noncredit uses of the workbook in school or public libraries, the instructor or librarian may want to provide the students with the answer sheets so that they can correct their own assignments. In these cases, the instruction sheets, assignment fill-in sheets, and answer sheets can be distributed to the students all in one packet.

3
Specific Suggestions

INSTRUCTIONAL PROCEDURES

The value of library research skills is not always readily apparent to students. The instructor may want to introduce the workbook with a discussion of student research needs and problems, and a discussion of the purposes of the workbook.

The time students should be given to complete the workbook depends on the course format. A semester is too long a period. Given too much time, students tend to fall behind, and then do several chapters in a rushed, short period of time. On the other hand, if given too little time students do not carefully read and digest the information; the results are usually careless mistakes in the assignments. The workbook should not be assigned during the last four weeks of any quarter or semester.

Because all students use the same titles to complete the assignments, there is a possibility that some students will have to wait while others use particular sources. This is especially likely if assignments are worked on during the class period. If students do the assignments during the class period, frustration over having to wait for the sources can be minimized by having them work on the questions in differing orders or, whenever possible, by having multiple copies of an assigned source.

At the start, students may have a tendency to try to complete the assignments without carefully reading both the text and the questions. The instructor should emphasize that the assignments can be done correctly and efficiently only after a careful reading of the material. The instructor should warn students about problems they may encounter if they do not examine the reference sources carefully. In some cases, the too casual student will find a partially correct answer but not the best answer for a question.

The organization of some sources, such as indexes and abstracts, is fairly complex. It is advisable to sup-plement the workbook and class discussion of those sources with transparencies and/or handouts demonstrating their use.

The fill-in sheets in Section VII should be photocopied for distribution to the students. If more than twenty students are enrolled in the course, some fill-in sheets will have to be given to more than one student. To forestall, if not prevent, students with the same sets identifying each other, the instructor may wish to modify the book numbers on the fill-in sheets so that they may be easily identified for grading purposes only.

Assignments should be corrected and returned to the students as quickly as possible. Immediate feedback is a requirement for optimal effectiveness of the manual as an instructional source. A system which allows students to hand in assignments as they complete them and pick up corrected exercises from a shelf in the library rather than during the class period has the advantage of providing immediate feedback, and further implements the library as laboratory concept.

Although the workbook can be graded on any basis, a pass/fail system is suggested since it provides a more relaxed atmosphere for the students and poses fewer problems of administration than other grading systems.

The assignments need not be corrected by a faculty member or professional librarian; however, those assignments which contain errors should be seen by the instructor or the librarian. In some cases, although the student may have used the source correctly, a careless mistake in writing down the answer could have been made. The instructor must decide how rigidly students will be held to supplying answers exactly as they appear on the answer sheets in Section VIII. There can be a fair amount of flexibility as to what will be accepted. The determinative test should be whether the student has demonstrated an understanding of how to use the source. Many questions ask the students to identify the page on which they found the information requested. This is generally asked to aid the instructor or reference librarian in determining why a student erred in locating the substantive information called for in the question. If the student provides the information correctly but not the page number, the instructor may decide that no useful educational purpose is served by having the student recheck the page number.

ROLE OF THE LIBRARY STAFF

The general reference staff can be very helpful to students if staff members are informed about plans for using the workbook, the schedule for the assignments, the nature of the questions, the exact location of the sources, and any special instructions given the students.

For students unfamiliar with the library, the staff may provide some initial general instruction about such things as the physical location of materials, the arrangement of the card catalogue and periodicals, and any special symbols or location devices used in the library.

Publications should be left on the shelves if they are part of a noncirculating collection, such as the reference collection, in order to provide the students with a realistic research environment. The work of the library staff will be kept to a minimum if the materials do not have to be handled by the reserve staff every time students use them. However, for publications in the general stacks and other publications whose use involves long delays before they are returned to the shelves (periodicals for example), the reserve collection may be the only viable location.

To minimize student frustration, it is essential that publications, other than those in the reserve collection, be on the shelves in their proper location. Circulation and reference staffs should be provided with a list of the titles and classification numbers of these publications, and asked to watch for them to insure their return as quickly as possible after use. It may be of help to tag or mark publications with a colored tape to indicate to staff that these are materials that should be reshelved immediately. If they are accidently misshelved, they are likely to be noticed more quickly if they are marked.

SOURCES

The library's holdings should be checked using the alphabetical list of annotated sources in Section VI. For books and indexes, the edition and/or volumes used in questions are identified. Journals are cited by the year, volume, and/or issue number. If a publication annotated in this workbook is not owned by the library and a decision is made not to purchase it, an appropriate publication, annotation, and question can be substituted.

If large numbers of students (more than 20-25 at a time) will be using the workbook, the instructor may want to have the library provide additional copies of some publications. Large groups can be accomodated without multiple copies, but this may require additional preparation and planning.

New editions of reference works may cause some problems for instructors using the fill-ins and answers supplied in Sections VII and VIII. In some cases, only the page number of the answer will change. In other cases, yearbooks for example, the information requested may be unavailable or changed in the new editions. Therefore, if a new edition of a source is used, the questions will have to be checked and correct answers substituted on the answer sheets in Section VIII. Old editions may be kept on the reference shelves for several years to reduce the frequency of changes in questions and answers required by changes in editions. If this procedure is used, students should be warned to use the appropriate editions.

When a publication for which there is an assignment cannot be located, the instructor may opt for any one of several alternative procedures. Students can be asked to use the publication in another library; a substitute question can be prepared; in cases where questions are taken from several volumes of a source and only one volume is missing, students can be provided with different fill-ins; or, the question can always be dropped. Multiple copies of one-volume works would, of course, eliminate the problem. Students could also be told that there will be no excuse accepted for not completing an assignment in an effort to obviate the possibility that publications will disappear while the course is in progress.

4
Instructor's Checklist

1. Check the sources annotated in the workbook against the holdings of your library. Be sure your library owns the issues or editions used in the questions. Section VI contains an alphabetical list of the sources, with the appropriate issues or editions specified.

2. For distribution to the students, prepare a list of the publications for which there are questions and place the call numbers for the publications on the list. You may want to arrange the publications in alphabetical order by title or list them by chapter. A sample list is contained in Section V.

3. Prepare instruction packets for the students. Section V contains a sample of instructions. Be sure to include:
   a. a question fill-in sheet, with instructions to write the sheet number and the fill-ins on the assignment pages in the manual;
   b. a schedule for the assignments;
   c. information about the grading system; and
   d. special instructions regarding such things as the turning in and returning of assignments, and publications which have been placed in the reserve collection or in other special locations in the library.

4. Make necessary arrangements regarding the publications which must be placed on reserve, moved, or in some way marked.

5. Notify the reference, circulation, and cataloging staffs in writing about the instruction program and any special procedures they should follow while the workbook is in use. Provide them with copies of the instructions given to the students.

6. Provide a copy of the workbook to the reference staff so that staff members may examine it before they are approached for help by students working on their assignments.

7. Prepare a student evaluation form for feedback about the usefulness of this instructional program and suggestions on ways in which procedures and materials can be made more effective.

8. Prepare a list of criteria that will be used in evaluating the student bibliographies and research "logs." These criteria should be communicated to the students in the instruction sheets (see the sample in Section V).

9. Prepare a grade sheet to record completed assignments for each student. For each assignment, record the date of completion. Be sure that the number for the set of question fill-ins and answers assigned to each student is recorded next to the student's name. This will allow you to be sure that students do not turn in answers to fill-ins not their own on a particular assignment and will enable you to replace correctly and easily their fill-in sheet should they lose it.

5
Samples of Materials for Distribution to Students During the First Class Period

The sample set of instructions on the following pages includes a schedule for completing the workbook based on a semester course meeting twice a week, as well as details on the assignments and how they can be graded. A sample list of courses has also been provided with call numbers. It is arranged to facilitate student use of the workbook.

6
Checklist of Titles Used in Assignments

This list is provided to facilitate checking the holdings of your library against the titles used in the assignments. Please pay particular attention to the date of the edition for each title. The answers provided in Section VIII are taken from the editions specified in this checklist.

America: History and Life. Santa Barbara, Calif.: American Bibliographical Center—Clio Press, vol. 1-. 1964/65.
    —1976 edition
American Historical Review. Washington, D. C.: American Historical Association, 1895-.
    —vol. 71, nos. 1, 3
    —vol. 72, nos. 2, 4
    —vol. 73, nos. 1, 4
    —vol. 74, nos. 1, 3
    —vol. 75, nos. 3, 5
Atlas of American History. Adams, James Truslow, ed. New York: Scribner, 1943.
Ayer Directory of Publications. Philadelphia: Ayer, 1880-. (Formerly titled *N. W. Ayer and Son's Directory of Newspapers and Periodicals.*)
    —1977 edition
Bibliographic Index. New York: Wilson, 1937-.
    —1974 cumulative edition
    —1975 cumulative edition
    —1976 cumulative edition
Cambridge Economic History of Europe. Cambridge, England: University Pr. 1941-1966.
Cumulative Subject Index to the Monthly Catalog of United States Government Publications 1900-1971. Washington, D.C.: Carrollton, 1973.
Dictionary of American Biography. New York: Scribner, 1928-37. 20 vols. and Index. Supplements 1-4. New York: Scribner, 1944-1974.
Dictionary of American History. Adams, James T.,

Continued on p. 13

<u>S A M P L E</u>

INSTRUCTIONS

<u>Assignments</u>

The assignments in this workbook are individualized. No two students in the class are asked to look up the same item of information. Attached are the fill-in portions of the questions. This set is unique to you. Please write your name and the number of the set on the cover, title page, and on each assignment page of your workbook. Then, for each assignment, write the fill-ins on the underlined spaces in the questions. Staple the fill-in sheet to the back cover of your workbook; you may want to refer to it later to insure that all information was copied correctly.

<u>Schedule</u>

The following is a schedule of due dates for all assignments. You may work ahead, but please avoid falling behind. Assignments may be turned in during the class period, or you may place them anytime in the bin marked "Deposit Workbooks Here," next to the Information Desk. The corrected copies will be placed on the "Pick Up Workbooks Here" shelves, also next to the Information Desk. They will be arranged alphabetically by your last name.

September 15	Chapters 1 - 2
September 20	Chapters 3 - 4
September 22	Chapters 5 - 6
September 27	Chapters 7 - 8
September 29	Chapters 9 - 10
October 4	Chapters 11 - 12
October 11	Chapter 13 + Bibliography

S A M P L E

Grading

The workbook will be administered on a complete/incomplete basis. Each assignment will be checked and errors will be identified. Credit will not be given for an assignment until all questions have been answered correctly.

The final assignment, the preparation of a bibliography and a journal recording the steps taken and sources used in the research, must be completed to the satisfaction of your instructor and the librarian.

The bibliography will be checked against the following criteria:

1. The appropriateness of the titles cited as sources of information for a research paper in an advanced history course. Factors which will be considered include the authors' reputations, the copyright dates, the publishers' reputations, the reputation of the journals.

2. The appropriateness of the titles cited as sources for the specific topic being researched.

3. The number of titles cited. Although the suitable number of titles will vary from subject to subject, a bibliography of less than fifteen titles raises, in most cases, the question of completeness.

4. The correctness of the bibliographic citation forms.

The journal should reflect the use of a reasonable variety of reference sources in the research. There must be a sound reason given in the journal for consulting each reference source.

S A M P L E

Special Information

Please read carefully the "Note to the Student" section in your workbook. If you follow the suggested procedures, your work will be much less burdensome. Also, keep the following in mind:

1. Only those sources which are annotated in the workbook have questions in the assignment section of each chapter.

2. All publications, except the scholarly journals and book review journals, will be found according to the classi-fication numbers provided on the attached list.

3. The scholarly journals and book review journals will be kept at the Reserve Desk.

<u>S A M P L E</u>

LIST OF SOURCES WITH LIBRARY OF CONGRESS CALL NUMBERS

<u>Chapter 1 - Guides to the Literature</u>

Guide to Historical Literature
REF. Z 6201 A55

Guide to Reference Books
REF. Z 1035.1 S43 1976

Harvard Guide to American History
REF. Z 1236 F77 1974

The Historian's Handbook
REF. Z 6201 P65

<u>Chapter 2 - Handbooks</u>

Encyclopedia of American History
REF. E 174.5 M847 1976

Encyclopedia of World History
REF. D 21 L27 1972

Historical Statistics of the United States
REF. HA 202 A385 1975

<u>Chapter 3 - Yearbooks and Almanacs</u>

Statesman's Yearbook: Statistical and Historical Annual of
the States of the World
REF. JA 51 S7

Statistical Abstract of the United States
REF. HA 202 A38

Statistical Yearbook
REF. HA 12.5 U63 1975

Whitaker's Almanack
REF. AY 754 W5

World Almanac
REF. AY 67 N5W7

<u>Chapter 4 - Atlases</u>

Atlas of American History
REF. G 1201 S1A2 1943

Historical Atlas
REF. G 1030 S4

Historical Atlas of the United States
REF. G 1201 S1L6 1969

Chapter 5 - Subject Dictionaries and Encyclopedias

Cambridge Economic History of Europe
REF. HC 240 C312

Dictionary of American History
REF. E 174 A43 1976

New Cambridge Modern History
REF. D 208 N4

Chapter 6 - Biographical Dictionaries

Dictionary of American Biography
REF. CT 213 D56

Dictionary of National Biography
REF. CT 773 D47

Directory of American Scholars
REF. CT 7040 C32

Webster's Biographical Dictionary
REF. CT 103 W4 1967

Chapter 7 - Indexes and Abstracts

America: History and Life
IND. Z 1236 A48

Historical Abstracts
IND. D 299 H51 & 52

Humanities Index
IND. AI 3 S612

Chapter 8 - Bibliographies

Bibliographic Index
IND. Z 1002 B595

Subject Catalog; A Cumulative List of Works Represented by
    Library of Congress Printed Cards
CAT. Z 881 A1 C325

Sample

A World Bibliography of Bibliographies and of Bibliographical
Catalogues, Calendars, Abstracts, Digests, Indexes and the Like
REF. Z 1002 B5685

Chapter 9 - Scholarly Journals

American Historical Review
On Reserve

Journal of American History
On Reserve

Magazines for Libraries
REF./OFF. Z 6941 K2 1972

Chapter 10 - Evaluating Book-Length Studies

History: Reviews of New Books
On Reserve

Reviews in American History
On Reserve

Chapter 11 - Newspapers

Ayer Directory of Publications
REF./OFF. Z 6951 A97 1977

New York Times Index
IND. AI N452

Times Index (London)
IND. AI 21 T462

Chapter 12 - Government Publications

Cumulative Subject Index to the Monthly Catalog of United
States Government Publications 1900-1971
IND. Z 1223 Z7B8

Government Publications: A Guide to Bibliographic Tools
REF. Z 7164 G7C5 1975

Monthly Catalog of United States Government Publications
IND. Z 1223 A18

Monthly Checklist of State Publications
IND. Z 1223.5 A1U5

ed. Rev. ed. New York: Scribner, 1976.

Dictionary of National Biography. London: Elder, 1908-09. 22 vols. 2nd-7th supplements. Oxford: University Pr., 1912-71. 6 vols.
—Main set used

Directory of American Scholars. 6th ed. New York: Bowker, 1974.

Encyclopedia of American History. Morris, Richard B. and Jeffrey B. Morris. New York: Harper, 1976.

Encyclopedia of World History. 5th ed. Langer, William. Boston: Houghton, 1972.

Government Publications: A Guide to Bibliographic Tools. 4th ed. Palic, Vladimir M. Washington, D. C.: Library of Congress, 1975.

Guide to Historical Literature. American Historical Association. New York: Macmillan, 1961.
—1967 edition

Guide to Reference Books. 9th ed. Sheehy, Eugene P. Chicago: American Library Association, 1976.

Harvard Guide to American History. Freidel, Frank, ed. Rev. ed. Cambridge: Harvard University Pr., 1974.
—v. 2

The Historian's Handbook: A Descriptive Guide to Reference Works. Poulton, Helen J. Norman: University of Oklahoma Pr., 1972.

Historical Abstracts. Santa Barbara, Calif.: American Bibliographical Center—Clio Press, vol. 1-. 1955-.
—1971 edition
—1972 edition
—1973 edition
—1974 edition

Historical Atlas. 9th ed. Shepard, William. New York: Barnes & Noble, 1965 (rpt. with rev., 1967).

Historical Statistics of the United States; Colonial Times to 1970. Washington, D. C.: Government Printing Office, 1976.

History: Reviews of New Books. Washington, D.C.: Johns Hopkins University Pr., 1972-.
—vol. 3, nos. 5, 7, 8, 10
—vol. 4, nos. 1, 2, 3, 4, 6, 7, 8, 9, 10
—vol. 5, nos. 1, 4, 5, 6, 7, 8

Humanities Index. New York: Wilson, vol. 1-. 1974/75.
—vol. 1, 1974-75
—vol. 2, 1975-76

Journal of American History. (Formerly *Mississippi Valley Historical Review.*) Bloomington, Indiana: Organization of American Historians, 1914-.
—vol. 55, no. 1
—vol. 56, no. 1

—vol. 57, nos. 1, 3
—vol. 58, nos. 1, 3
—vol. 59, nos. 1, 3
—vol. 60, nos. 1, 3

Magazines for Libraries. 2nd ed. Katz, William. New York: Bowker, 1972.

Monthly Catalog of United States Government Publications. U. S. Superintendent of Documents. Washington, D. C.: Government Printing Office, 1885-.
—1949
—1951
—1954
—1956
—1957
—1960
—1961
—1963
—1965
—1966
—1967
—1968
—1969

Monthly Checklist of State Publications. U. S. Library of Congress. Washington, D. C.: Government Printing Office, 1910-.
—1972
—1974
—1975

New Cambridge Modern History. Cambridge, England: University Pr., 1957-1970.

New York Times Index. New York: The New York Times, 1913-.
—1970
—1971
—1972

Reviews in American History. Westport, Conn.: Redgrave Information Resources Corp., 1973-.
—vol. 2, nos. 3, 4
—vol. 3, nos. 1, 2, 3, 4
—vol. 4, nos. 1, 2, 3, 4

Statesman's Yearbook: Statistical and Historical Annual of the States of the World. New York: St. Martin's, 1864-.
—1976-77 edition

Statistical Abstract of the United States. Washington, D. C.: Government Printing Office, 1879-.
—1976 edition

Statistical Yearbook. United Nations. Statistical Office. New York: 1949-.
—1975 edition

Subject Catalog; A Cumulative List of Works Represented by Library of Congress Printed Cards. U. S. Library of Congress. Washington, D. C.:

1950-. (Formerly titled *Books: Subjects*).
—1965-69
—1970-74
—1975
Times Index. Times, London (Indexes). Reading, England: Newspaper Archive Developments Limited, 1906-.
  —September-October 1967
  —November-December 1967
  —March-April 1968
  —September-October 1968
  —January-February 1969
  —March-April 1969
  —September-October 1969
  —January-February 1970
  —May-June 1971
  —January-March 1972
  —April-June 1972
  —July-September 1972

—October-December 1972
—July-September 1973
—January-March 1974
—July-September 1974
—October-December 1974
—January-March 1975
—April-June 1975
—July-September 1976
Webster's Biographical Dictionary. Springfield, Mass.: Merriam, 1967.
Whitaker's Almanack. London: J. Whitaker, 1869-.
  —1977 edition
World Almanac. New York: World-Telegram, 1868-.
  —1977 edition
A World Bibliography of Bibliographies and of Bibliographical Catalogs, Calendars, Abstracts, Digests, Indexes and the Like. 4th ed. Besterman, Theodore A. Lausanne: Societas Bibliographica, 1965-66.

7
Assignment Fill-In Sheets

Copies of the fill-in sheets provided on the following pages should be distributed to the students with instructions to: (1) write the fill-in sheet number (which appears on the upper right hand corner) on each assignment page of their workbooks; (2) write the appropriate information in the underlined spaces provided for each question; and (3) staple the fill-in sheets to the back cover of the workbook for future reference. The "Q" indicates question numbers in assignments.

MATERIALS & METHODS
FOR
HISTORY RESEARCH

Fill-ins by Book

Book No. __1__

CHAPTER ONE

Q.1. an American literature survey course
Q.3. a guide to the study of medieval history
Q.4. Medieval Western Europe
feudalism
Q.5. the Federalist Era
the rise of political parties

CHAPTER TWO

Q.2. 1940
Q.3. Sept. 7, 1916
Q.4. late nineteenth century diplomacy
a. Who were the signatories of the Suez
Canal Convention of 1888

CHAPTER THREE

Q.2. Chile
Q.3. a. Alabama
Q.4. Latin American
a. Brazil
(Use the 1975 edition.)
Q.5. Nov. 12, 1975
Q.6. Aberdare

CHAPTER FOUR

Q.2. Battle of Alamance
Q.3. corn in 1840
Q.4. Ancient Egypt

CHAPTER FIVE

Q.2. tithingmen
Q.3. the agrarian life of the Middle Ages
the evolution of agriculture technique
Q.4. 1713-1763
international relationships

CHAPTER SIX

Q.2. Antoine Arnauld
Q.3. David Abercromby
Q.4. William Yates Atkinson
Q.5. Thomas Wilson Africa

CHAPTER SEVEN

Q.3. the American Civil War
refugee camps
Q.4. the Indian removal policy in Kansas
(1816-1860)
Q.5. Communism in Algeria
1974

CHAPTER EIGHT

Q.2. the Arab countries
1976
Q.3. the history of modern Italy
the career of Gabriele d'Annunzio
Q.4. Battle of Agincourt
1970-74

CHAPTER NINE

Q.2. American Historical Review
vol. 71, no. 3, April 1966
a. "The Middle Class in West. Europe
1815-1848"
b. Bently B. Gilbert
c. About what 1911 law is the author
writing?
d. Reformer in Modern China: Chang Chien,
1853-1929
Q.3. Alabama

CHAPTER TEN

Q.2. The Shaping of Southern Politics: Suffrage
Restriction and the Establishment of the
One-Party South, 1880-1910
J. Morgan Kousser
Q.3. British Slave Emancipation: The Sugar
Colonies and the Great Experiment, 1830-
1865
William A. Green
v. 4, no. 10, September 1976
Q.4. Seven Who Shaped Our Destiny: The Founding
Fathers as Revolutionaries
Richard B. Morris
v. 2, no. 3, September 1974

CHAPTER ELEVEN

Q.2. Algoma
Q.3. Niger Republic
1972
Q.4. a. May-June 1971

CHAPTER TWELVE

Q.2. Maine
1975
Q.3. Alaska
Q.4. the Supreme Command in the European Theatre

MATERIALS & METHODS
FOR
HISTORY RESEARCH

Fill-ins by Book

Book No. 2

CHAPTER ONE

Q.2. an introductory anthropology course
Q.3. a bibliography on the history of Great
     Britain
Q.4. Medieval Western Europe
     chivalry
Q.5. the Federalist Era
     developments on the frontier

CHAPTER TWO

Q.2. 1941
Q.3. Nov. 18, 1903
Q.4. the Nazi movement
     a. Who was the general who aided Hitler
        during the Beer Hall Putsch

CHAPTER THREE

Q.2. Colombia
Q.3. a. Alaska
Q.4. African
     a. Chad
     (Use the 1975 edition.)
Q.5. Nov. 21, 1975
Q.6. Argyll

CHAPTER FOUR

Q.2. Battle of Bear River
Q.3. corn in 1860
Q.4. Mycenean Greece

CHAPTER FIVE

Q.2. the Richmond junto
Q.3. the agrarian life of the Middle Ages
     the settlement and colonization of Europe
Q.4. 1715-1763
     the development of the visual arts

CHAPTER SIX

Q.2. Italo Balbo
Q.3. Thomas Bodley
Q.4. Henry Whitney Bellows
Q.5. Oscar Theodore Barck

CHAPTER SEVEN

Q.3. U.S. diplomatic history
     causes of the Korean war
Q.4. Jim Crow laws in Arkansas
Q.5. nationalism in Nigeria
     1974

CHAPTER EIGHT

Q.2. Asia
     1976
Q.3. English social and cultural history
     the career and writings of James Boswell
Q.4. Hundred Years' War
     1970-74

CHAPTER NINE

Q.2. American Historical Review
     vol. 72, no. 4, July 1967
     a. "Early Mesopotamian Constitutional
        Development"
     b. Irwin Unger
     c. When did the cited article on American
        consensus by John Higham appear
     d. Makers of Modern England: The Force of
        Individual Genius in History
Q.3. Alaska

CHAPTER TEN

Q.2. Ethnic Alienation: The Italian-American
     P. J. Gallo
Q.3. The Rise of German Industrial Power, 1834-
     1914
     W. O. Henderson
     v. 4, no. 9, August 1976
Q.4. Five Public Philosophies of Walter Lippman
     Benjamin F. Wright
     v. 2, no. 4, December 1974

CHAPTER ELEVEN

Q.2. Janesville
Q.3. Nigeria
     1972
Q.4. a. January-March 1972

CHAPTER TWELVE

Q.2. Hawaii
     1975
Q.3. Arkansas
Q.4. the German anti-guerrilla operation in
     the Balkans

MATERIALS & METHODS
FOR
HISTORY RESEARCH

Fill-ins by Book

Book No. ___3___

CHAPTER ONE

Q.2. an astronomy course
Q.3. a bibliography on the history of the Far
     East
Q.4. Medieval Western Europe
     the Crusades
Q.5. Jacksonian democracy
     reform movements

CHAPTER TWO

Q.2. 1942
Q.3. Mar. 9, 1841
Q.4. Nazi Germany
     a. Who were the three German political
        parties that voted for the Enabling
        Act in 1933

CHAPTER THREE

Q.2. El Salvador
Q.3. a. Arkansas
Q.4. Latin American
     a. Chile
     (Use the 1975 edition.)
Q.5. Jan. 9, 1976
Q.6. Basingstoke

CHAPTER FOUR

Q.2. Battle of Bad Axe
Q.3 corn in 1890
Q.4. The Assyrian Empire

CHAPTER FIVE

Q.2. the Patriot War (1837-38)
Q.3. the agrarian life of the Middle Ages
     the rise of dependent cultivation and
        seignorial institutions
Q.4. 1609-1659
     the Thirty Years' War

CHAPTER SIX

Q.2. Francisco García Calderón
Q.3. John Bunyan
Q.4. William Evelyn Cameron
Q.5. John Garretson Clark

CHAPTER SEVEN

Q.3. the Reformation
     the German Peasant's War (1524-1525)
Q.4. the Spanish-Indian relations in California
        missions 1750-1850
Q.5. revolutions and revolutionary movements in
        Zaire
     1974

CHAPTER EIGHT

Q.2. Australia
     1976
Q.3. the development of political theory in
        Europe
     the career and writing of Edmund Burke
Q.4. Battle of Bosworth Field
     1970-74

CHAPTER NINE

Q.2. American Historical Review
     v. 74, no. 1, Oct. 1968
     a. "The Perils of Pluralism: the Background
        of the Pierce Case"
     b. Andrew C. Hess
     c. Who wrote the cited article The
        Structure of Spanish History
     d. Rebels of the Woods: the I. W. W. in the
        Pacific Northwest
Q.3. Illinois

CHAPTER TEN

Q.2. Making of the TVA
     A. E. Morgan
Q.3. The Critical Phase in Tanzania 1945-1968
        Nyerere and the Emergence of a Socialist
        Strategy
     Cranford Pratt
     v. 4, no. 8, July 1976
Q.4. Free Men All: The Personal Liberty Laws of
        the North 1780-1861
     Thomas D. Morris
     v. 2, no. 4, December 1974

CHAPTER ELEVEN

Q.2. Marshfield
Q.3. Ghana
     1972
Q.4. a. October-December 1972

CHAPTER TWELVE

Q.2. Louisiana
     1975
Q.3. California
Q.4. Stalingrad to Berlin, the German defeat in
        the East

MATERIALS & METHODS
FOR
HISTORY RESEARCH

Fill-ins by Book

Book No. ___4___

CHAPTER ONE

Q.2. an introductory economics course
Q.3. an encyclopedia of the social sciences
Q.4. Medieval Western Europe
     papal government
Q.5. Jacksonian democracy
     the Taney Court

CHAPTER TWO

Q.2. 1943
Q.3. Aug. 9, 1842
Q.4. France in the 1930s
     a. Who were the three major political
        parties which were part of, or
        supported, the Popular Front
        Government in France

CHAPTER THREE

Q.2. Guatemala
Q.3. a. Florida
Q.4. Latin American
     a. Colombia
     (Use the 1975 edition.)
Q.5. Jan. 19, 1976
Q.6. Birkenhead

CHAPTER FOUR

Q.2. Battle of San Gabriel
Q.3. corn in 1920
Q.4. Ancient Palestine

CHAPTER FIVE

Q.2. Lind's Mission to Mexico
Q.3. the agrarian life of the Middle Ages
     agrarian institutions of the Germanic
        Kingdoms
Q.4. 1609-1659
     Sweden and the Baltic

CHAPTER SIX

Q.2. Ferencz Deák
Q.3. William Chillingworth
Q.4. Frederick Morgan Crunden
Q.5. Richard Slator Dunn

CHAPTER SEVEN

Q.3. the history of World War II
     the 1944 battle of Warsaw
Q.4. the Creek War in Alabama
Q.5. revolutions and revolutionary movements in
        Uganda
     1974

CHAPTER EIGHT

Q.2. China
     1976
Q.3. early American history
     the career of Aaron Burr
Q.4. Battle of Marston Moor
     1970-74

CHAPTER NINE

Q.2. American Historical Review
     vol. 73, no. 1, October 1967
     a. "The Serbian Campaign of 1915: Its
        Diplomatic Background"
     b. James T. Patterson
     c. To what source does the author refer
        the reader for a description of new
        federalism? Give complete citation.
     d. Architecture in Ancient Egypt and the
        Near East
Q.3. Iowa

CHAPTER TEN

Q.2. Frontier Violence: Another Look
     W. Eugene Hollon
Q.3. The King's Council in the Reign of
        Edward VI
     D. E. Hoak
     v. 5, no. 1, October 1976
Q.4. The New Heavens and New Earth: Political
        Religion in America
     Cushing Strout
     v. 3, no. 1, March 1975

CHAPTER ELEVEN

Q.2. Baldwin
Q.3. Tanzania
     1972
Q.4. a. January-March 1974

CHAPTER TWELVE

Q.2. Michigan
     1975
Q.3. Colorado
Q.4. the U.S. Pacific victory at Okinawa

MATERIALS & METHODS
FOR
HISTORY RESEARCH

Fill-ins by Book

Book No. ___5___

CHAPTER ONE

Q.2. an English literature survey course
Q.3. an encyclopedia or dictionary of United
     States history
Q.4. Medieval Western Europe
     monasticism
Q.5. the Civil War
     the causes of the conflict

CHAPTER TWO

Q.2. 1944
Q.3. July 3, 1844
Q.4. the cold war
     a. What was the formal name for the Manila
        Pact and the immediate event that
        caused its formation

CHAPTER THREE

Q.2. Guinea
Q.3. a. Georgia
Q.4. European
     a. Denmark
     (Use the 1975 edition.)
Q.5. Jan. 24, 1976
Q.6. Blyth

CHAPTER FOUR

Q.2. Battle of Salt Creek
Q.3. corn in 1950
Q.4. Historic Greece (700-600 B.C.)

CHAPTER FIVE

Q.2. the Mississippi Bubble
Q.3. the Industrial Revolution
     the transformation of European agriculture
Q.4. 1559-1610
     the Austrian Habsburgs and the Empire

CHAPTER SIX

Q.2. Johann Eck
Q.3. Richard Crashaw
Q.4. Samuel Train Dutton
Q.5. Erling A. Erickson

CHAPTER SEVEN

Q.3. Chinese history
     the Sung Dynasty
Q.4. Jacob Hamblin and the Mountain Meadows
        Massacre in Utah
Q.5. Communism in Tanzania
     1974

CHAPTER EIGHT

Q.2. France
     1976
Q.3. English social and cultural history
     the career of Samuel Butler
Q.4. Battle of the Nile (1798)
     1970-74

CHAPTER NINE

Q.2. American Historical Review
     vol. 71, no. 1, October 1965
     a. "King's Friends, Civil Servants, or
        Politicians"
     b. Frank W. Iklé
     c. Who was the German ambassador in Peking
        in January 1915
     d. Government and People in Hong Kong, 1841-
        1962: A Constitutional History
Q.3. Wyoming

CHAPTER TEN

Q.2. The Other South: Southern Dissenters in the
        Nineteenth Century
     Carl N. Degler
Q.3. Hitler Among the Germans
     Rudolph Binion
     v. 5, no. 7, May/June 1977
Q.4. The Abolitionists: The Growth of a
        Dissenting Minority
     Merton C. Dillon
     v. 3, no. 3, September 1975

CHAPTER ELEVEN

Q.2. Chetek
Q.3. Tunisia
     1972
Q.4. a. July-September 1974

CHAPTER TWELVE

Q.2. New Jersey
     1975
Q.3. Connecticut
Q.4. the liberation of Belgrade in 1944

MATERIALS & METHODS
FOR
HISTORY RESEARCH

Fill-ins by Book

Book No.   6

CHAPTER ONE

Q.2. an introductory business course
Q.3. an encyclopedia or dictionary of the
     history of Great Britain
Q.4. Medieval Western Europe
     an economic topic, specifically the
     agrarian economy of Medieval Europe
Q.5. the Civil War
     the military history of the conflict

CHAPTER TWO

Q.2. 1945
Q.3. June 15, 1846
Q.4. early nineteenth century diplomacy
     a. When was the German Act of Confederation
        signed

CHAPTER THREE

Q.2. Haiti
Q.3. Hawaii
Q.4. European
     a. Finland
     (Use the 1975 edition.)
Q.5. Feb. 10, 1976
Q.6. Chelmsford

CHAPTER FOUR

Q.2. Battle of Resaca
Q.3. cotton in 1840
Q.4. Oriental Empires about 600 B.C.

CHAPTER FIVE

Q.2. the Fetterman Massaore
Q.3. the economy of Europe in the sixteenth and
     seventeenth centuries
     prices in Europe from 1450 to 1750
Q.4. 1688-1725
     the scientific movement

CHAPTER SIX

Q.2. Juan Fernández
Q.3. Dud Dudley
Q.4. Charles Benjamin Farwell
Q.5. Kent Forster

CHAPTER SEVEN

Q.3. Chinese history
     the Tartar conquest of China (1643-1644)
Q.4. the "Suicide Fight" of the Northern
     Cheyenne Indians in Montana
Q.5. urbanization in Ghana
     1973

CHAPTER EIGHT

Q.2. Great Britain
     1976
Q.3. Afro-American history
     the career of George Washington Carver
Q.4. Battle of Marengo
     1970-74

CHAPTER NINE

Q.2. American Historical Review
     vol. 72, no. 2, January 1967
     a. "Jacopo Aconcio as an Engineer"
     b. George V. Taylor
     c. In what city was an earlier version of
        this article read
     d. Ancient India: A History of Its Culture
        and Civilization
Q.3. Arizona

CHAPTER TEN

Q.2. Fur Trade in Colonial New York 1686-1776
     Thomas E. Norton
Q.3. Bismarck
     Alan Palmer
     v. 5, no. 8, July 1977
Q.4. Him/Her/Self: Sex Roles in Modern America
     Peter G. Filene
     v. 3, no. 4, December 1975

CHAPTER ELEVEN

Q.2. Amery
Q.3. Sierra Leone
     1972
Q.4. a. January-March 1975

CHAPTER TWELVE

Q.2. New York
     1975
Q.3. Delaware
Q.4. Japanese operations in the Southwest
     Pacific

MATERIALS & METHODS
FOR
HISTORY RESEARCH

Fill-ins by Book

Book No. ___7___

CHAPTER ONE

Q.2. an introductory chemistry course
Q.3. an encyclopedia of Australia and New
     Zealand
Q.4. Medieval Western Europe
     an economic topic, specifically on trade
     in Medieval Europe
Q.5. the Reconstruction Era
     radical reconstruction

CHAPTER TWO

Q.2. 1946
Q.3. Aug. 6, 1846
Q.4. the founding of the state of Israel
     a. Who was the government that issued the
        Balfour Declaration? What was the
        year? What issue did it treat

CHAPTER THREE

Q.2. Honduras
Q.3. a. Kentucky
Q.4. European
     a. Greece
     (Use the 1975 edition.)
Q.5. Feb. 24, 1976
Q.6. Darlington

CHAPTER FOUR

Q.2. Battle of Point Pleasant
Q.3. cotton in 1860
Q.4. The Persian Empire

CHAPTER FIVE

Q.2. Gold Democrats
Q.3. economic organization and policies in the
     Middle Ages
     public credit
Q.4. 1520-1559
     constitutional development and political
     thought in Eastern Europe

CHAPTER SIX

Q.2. Vasco da Gama
Q.3. Orlando Gibbons
Q.4. James Albert Gary
Q.5. Charles Garrett

CHAPTER SEVEN

Q.3. the American Revolution
     religious aspects of the American
     Revolution
Q.4. German-American communes in Missouri
Q.5. federation in Algeria
     1973

CHAPTER EIGHT

Q.2. Saudi Arabia
     1976
Q.3. the history of Communism
     Communism in Latin America
Q.4. Battle of Hastings
     1970-74

CHAPTER NINE

Q.2. American Historical Review
     vol. 75, no. 3, Feb. 1970
     a. "The Creation of Nobles in Prussia,
        1871-1918"
     b. Jerry Israel
     c. In what year was the cited article by
        Walter LaFeber ("America's Long Dream
        in Asia") published
     d. The Birth of Indian Civilization: India
        and Pakistan Before 500 B.C.
Q.3. Arkansas

CHAPTER TEN

Q.2. Politics of Populism: Dissent in Colorado
     James E. Wright
Q.3. The Secret Police in Lenin's Russia
     Lennard D. Gerson
     v. 5, no. 6, April 1977
Q.4. Decade of Disillusionment: The Kennedy
     Johnson Years
     Jim F. Heath
     v. 3, no. 4, December 1975

CHAPTER ELEVEN

Q.2. Mineral Point
Q.3. Dahomey
     1972
Q.4. a. January-February 1970

CHAPTER TWELVE

Q.2. North Carolina
     1975
Q.3. Florida
Q.4. the liberation of Guam

MATERIALS & METHODS
FOR
HISTORY RESEARCH

Fill-ins by Book

Book No. ___8___

CHAPTER ONE

Q.2. an introductory geography course
Q.3. a guide or index to biographical sources
Q.4. Medieval Western Europe
    an economic topic, specifically on money
        and banking in Medieval Europe
Q.5. the Gilded Age
    urban growth

CHAPTER TWO

Q.2. 1947
Q.3. Apr. 24, 1913
Q.4. Roman political history
    a. What was the major provision of the
        Edict of Caracalla

CHAPTER THREE

Q.2. Iran
Q.3. Louisiana
Q.4. European
    a. France
    (Use the 1975 edition.)
Q.5. Mar. 2, 1976
Q.6. Finchley

CHAPTER FOUR

Q.2. Battle of Olustee
Q.3. cotton in 1890
Q.4. Propontis

CHAPTER FIVE

Q.2. Cotton Money
Q.3. the agrarian life of the Middle Ages
    agriculture and rural life in the later
        Roman Empire
Q.4. 1520-1559
    Luther and the German Reformation to 1529

CHAPTER SIX

Q.2. Hugo Haase
Q.3. Jonathan Goddard
Q.4. Thomas Andrews Hendricks
Q.5. Michael Fitzgibbon Holt

CHAPTER SEVEN

Q.3. European colonialism
    the Dutch East India Company
Q.4. the Sand Creek Massacre in Colorado
Q.5. Ethiopia and World War II
    1973

CHAPTER EIGHT

Q.2. Canada
    1975
Q.3. American cultural history
    the career and writings of Henry Adams
Q.4. Battle of Poitiers (1356)
    1970-74

CHAPTER NINE

Q.2. American Historical Review
    vol. 75, no. 5, June 1970
    a. "The Domestic Policies of Peter III and
        His Overthrow"
    b. John Demos
    c. When was an earlier version of the
        article presented as a paper
    d. The Country Gentry in the Fourteenth
        Century: With Special Reference to the
        Heraldic Rolls of Arms
Q.3. California

CHAPTER TEN

Q.2. Too Proud to Fight: Woodrow Wilson's
        Neutrality
    Patrick Devlin
Q.3. Racism, Revolution, Reaction, 1861-1877
        The Rise and Fall of Radical
        Reconstruction
    Peter Camejo
    v. 5, no. 5, March 1977
Q.4. The Entrepreneurs: Explorations Within the
        American Business Tradition
    Robert Sobel
    v. 3, no. 3, September 1975

CHAPTER ELEVEN

Q.2. Elroy
Q.3. Mali
    1972
Q.4. a. September-October 1969

CHAPTER TWELVE

Q.2. Oregon
    1975
Q.3. Georgia
Q.4. the Ardennes (the Battle of the Bulge)

MATERIALS & METHODS
FOR
HISTORY RESEARCH

Fill-ins by Book

Book No.   9

CHAPTER ONE

Q.2. an introductory geology course
Q.3. a major English language world gazetteer
Q.4. Medieval Western Europe
     cultural developments, specifically on the
       development of philosophy
Q.5. the Gilded Age
     the development of business and the economy

CHAPTER TWO

Q.2. 1948
Q.3. June 18, 1910
Q.4. early twentieth century diplomatic history
     a. What were the years of the "Pig War"
          between Austria and Serbia

CHAPTER THREE

Q.2. Kuwait
Q.3. a. Nevada
Q.4. European
     a. Italy
     (Use the 1975 edition.)
Q.5. Mar. 9, 1976
Q.6. Inverness

CHAPTER FOUR

Q.2. Battle of Orchard Knob
Q.3. cotton in 1920
Q.4. Greek and Phoenician Settlements (550 B.C.)

CHAPTER FIVE

Q.2. the Dull Knife Campaign (1878-79)
Q.3. economic organization and policies in the
       Middle Ages
     the rise of the towns
Q.4. 1493-1520
     the Hispanic Kingdoms and the Catholic
       Kings

CHAPTER SIX

Q.2. Carlos Ibañez del Campo
Q.3. Denzil Holles
Q.4. Henry Rootes Jackson
Q.5. David Louis Jacobson

CHAPTER SEVEN

Q.3. the history of Latin America
     the British Honduras question
Q.4. slavery in Delaware
Q.5. foreign aid in Somalia
     1973

CHAPTER EIGHT

Q.2. Cuba
     1975
Q.3. the history of religions
     the history of Congregationalism
Q.4. Battle of Leipzig
     1970-74

CHAPTER NINE

Q.2. American Historical Review
     vol. 73, no. 4, April 1968
     a. "The Strategy of Southern Railroads"
     b. Andreas Dorpalen
     c. In what years did the unification
          movement take place?
     d. Competitive Interference and Twentieth
          Century Diplomacy
Q.3. Kansas

CHAPTER TEN

Q.2. Black Majority: Negroes in Colonial South
       Carolina from 1670 Through the Stono
       Rebellion
     Peter H. Wood
Q.3. The English People and the English
       Revolution 1640-1649
     Brian Manning
     v. 5, no. 4, February 1977
Q.4. The Other South: Southern Dissenters in the
       Nineteenth Century
     Carl N. Degler
     v. 3, no. 1, March 1975

CHAPTER ELEVEN

Q.2. Durand
Q.3. Zaire
     1972
Q.4. a. January-February 1969

CHAPTER TWELVE

Q.2. South Carolina
     1975
Q.3. Hawaii
Q.4. the assault on Peleliu

MATERIALS & METHODS
FOR
HISTORY RESEARCH

Fill-ins by Book

Book No. ___10___

CHAPTER ONE

Q.2. an introductory law course
Q.3. a regional biographical source with
     coverage limited to Africa
Q.4. Medieval Western Europe
     cultural developments, specifically on the
     development of political thought
Q.5. the Gilded Age
     American foreign relations

CHAPTER TWO

Q.2. 1949
Q.3. June 5, 1854
Q.4. religious history
     a. What is the name of the book published
        by Emanuel Swedenborg in 1758 which
        was a founding text for the Church of
        the New Jerusalem

CHAPTER THREE

Q.2. Morocco
Q.3. a. New Jersey
Q.4. African
     a. Kenya
     (Use the 1975 edition.)
Q.5. Mar. 16, 1976
Q.6. Maidstone

CHAPTER FOUR

Q.2. Battle of Hobkirk's Hill
Q.3. cotton in 1950
Q.4. Attica

CHAPTER FIVE

Q.2. the Bosque Redondo
Q.3. economic organization and policies in the
     Middle Ages
     the organization of trade
Q.4. 1493-1520
     learning and education in Western Europe

CHAPTER SIX

Q.2. Karl Johann Kautsky
Q.3. Inigo Jones
Q.4. James Frederick Joy
Q.5. Jay Kinsbruner

CHAPTER SEVEN

Q.3. the history of France
     the Edict of Nantes
Q.4. anti-German sentiment in Florida in the
     early 1900s
Q.5. political parties in Uganda
     1973

CHAPTER EIGHT

Q.2. Eastern Europe
     1975
Q.3. Medieval history
     the Crusades
Q.4. Battle of Marathon
     1970-74

CHAPTER NINE

Q.2. American Historical Review
     vol. 74, no. 3, February 1969
     a. "Racial Segregation in Ante Bellum New
        Orleans"
     b. Sheldon Hackney
     c. What was the "suicide-homicide ratio"
        for southern whites in 1964?
     d. Science and Civilization in Islam
Q.3. Maryland

CHAPTER TEN

Q.2. Red, White and Black: The Peoples of Early
     America
     Gary B. Nash
Q.3. The Death of Stalin
     Georges Bortoli
     v. 3, no. 8, July 1975
Q.4. A Compromise of Principle: Congressional
     Republicans and Reconstruction, 1863-1869
     Michael Les Benedict
     v. 3, no. 2, June 1975

CHAPTER ELEVEN

Q.2. Blanchardville
Q.3. Zambia
     1972
Q.4. a. March-April 1969

CHAPTER TWELVE

Q.2. Texas
     1975
Q.3. Illinois
Q.4. the China-Burma-India Theater of operations

MATERIALS & METHODS
FOR
HISTORY RESEARCH

Fill-ins by Book

Book No. __11__

CHAPTER ONE

Q.2. a mineralogy course
Q.3. a national biographical source with
       coverage limited to Australians
Q.4. Medieval Western Europe
       cultural developments, specifically on
       literature
Q.5. the Progressive Era
       the "Social Gospel"

CHAPTER TWO

Q.2. 1950
Q.3. Nov. 18, 1901
Q.4. religious history
       a. Who was the reigning pope when the dogma
           of the infalability of the papacy was
           proclaimed

CHAPTER THREE

Q.2. Nicaragua
Q.3. a. New York
Q.4. African
       a. Malawi
       (Use the 1975 edition.)
Q.5. Mar. 23, 1976
Q.6. Newark

CHAPTER FOUR

Q.2. Battle of French Creek
Q.3. tobacco in 1700
Q.4. the Macedonian Empire (336-323 B.C.)

CHAPTER FIVE

Q.2. the Atherton Company
Q.3. economic organization and policies in the
       Middle Ages
       the economic policies of towns
Q.4. 1830-1870
       the alliance system and the balance of
       power

CHAPTER SIX

Q.2. Louis Hypolite Lafontaine
Q.3. Godfrey Kneller
Q.4. Philip Ludwell
Q.5. John Tate Lanning

CHAPTER SEVEN

Q.3. European diplomatic history
       the Munich four power agreement
Q.4. the annexation of Hawaii
Q.5. Algerian border disputes
       1972

CHAPTER EIGHT

Q.2. Germany
       1975
Q.3. the history of American ethnic groups
       United States immigrants from Denmark
Q.4. Battle of Waterloo
       1965-69

CHAPTER NINE

Q.2. Journal of American History
       vol. 59, no. 1, June 1972
       a. "Slavery and Freedom: The American
           Paradox?"
       b. Robert A. Divine
       c. Whose assistance in supporting the
           research for the article was
           acknowledged
       d. The Naval Academy: Illustrated History
           of the United States Navy
Q.3. Montana

CHAPTER TEN

Q.2. A Nation in the Making: The Philippines and
       the United States, 1899-1921
       Peter W. Stanley
Q.3. France Under the Directory
       Martyn Lyons
       v. 4, no. 4, February 1976
Q.4. Peasants and Strangers: Italians, Rumanians,
       and Slovaks in an American City,
       1890-1950
       Josef J. Barton
       v. 4, no. 1, March 1976

CHAPTER ELEVEN

Q.2. Horicon
Q.3. Ghana
       1971
Q.4. a. September-October 1967

CHAPTER TWELVE

Q.2. Washington
       1975
Q.3. Indiana
Q.4. the Brazilian Expeditionary Force in the
       Italian Campaign

MATERIALS & METHODS
FOR
HISTORY RESEARCH

Fill-ins by Book

Book No. __12__

CHAPTER ONE

Q.2. an introductory music course
Q.3. an occupational biographical source with
     coverage limited to the American Congress
Q.4. Medieval Western Europe
     cultural developments, specifically on art
Q.5. the Progressive Era
     the development of business and the economy

CHAPTER TWO

Q.2. 1951
Q.3. May 22, 1872
Q.4. twentieth century German political history
     a. Who were the two leaders of the German
        Spartacists

CHAPTER THREE

Q.2. Pakistan
Q.3. a. North Dakota
Q.4. African
     a. Morocco
     (Use the 1975 edition.)
Q.5. Mar. 4, 1976
Q.6. Normanton

CHAPTER FOUR

Q.2. Battle of Black Jack
Q.3. tobacco in 1775
Q.4. Rome and Carthage (218 B.C.)

CHAPTER FIVE

Q.2. the Burke Act of 1906
Q.3. economic organization and policies in the
        Middle Ages
     the Gilds
Q.4. 1830-1870
     liberalism and constitutional development

CHAPTER SIX

Q.2. Louis Jean Malvy
Q.3. Henry Blosse Lynch
Q.4. Christopher Gustavus Memminger
Q.5. Joseph James Malone

CHAPTER SEVEN

Q.3. European diplomatic history
     the Crimean War
Q.4. colonial courts in Massachusetts
Q.5. industrialization in Nigeria
     1972

CHAPTER EIGHT

Q.2. Great Britain
     1975
Q.3. the history of American ethnic groups
     United States immigrants from Mexico
Q.4. Battle of Trafalgar
     1965-69

CHAPTER NINE

Q.2. Journal of American History
     vol. 60, no. 1, June 1973
     a. "Religious Benevolence as Social Control:
        a Critique of an Interpretation"
     b. Allan Peskin
     c. In what year did the cited book by
        James P. Shenton (The Reconstruction:
        A Documentary History of the South
        after the War: 1865-1877) appear?
     d. American Enterprise: Free and Not So
        Free?
Q.3. North Dakota

CHAPTER TEN

Q.2. Americans in Conflict: The Civil War and
        Reconstruction
     David Lindsey
Q.3. Democracy and Organization in the Chinese
        Industrial Enterprise (1948-1953)
     William Brugger
     v. 4, no. 8, July 1976
Q.4. The Presidency of John Adams
     Ralph Adams Brown
     v. 4, no. 4, December 1976

CHAPTER ELEVEN

Q.2. Barron
Q.3. Tanzania
     1971
Q.4. a. March-April 1968

CHAPTER TWELVE

Q.2. West Virginia
     1975
Q.3. Iowa
Q.4. the Soviet partisan movement 1941-44

MATERIALS & METHODS
FOR
HISTORY RESEARCH

Fill-ins by Book

Book No. __13__

CHAPTER ONE

Q.2. an introductory philosophy course
Q.3. an occupational biographical source with
     coverage limited to the justices of the
     U.S. Supreme Court
Q.4. the Roman Republic and Empire
     Roman military history
Q.5. World War II
     wartime diplomacy

CHAPTER TWO

Q.2. 1952
Q.3. Feb. 3, 1887
Q.4. eighteenth century diplomatic history
     a. Who did the Russians defeat in the
        Battle of Grossjägerndorf

CHAPTER THREE

Q.2. Qatar
Q.3. a. Oklahoma
Q.4. European
     a. Netherlands
     (Use the 1975 edition.)
Q.5. Mar. 12, 1976
Q.6. Pontypool

CHAPTER FOUR

Q.2. Battle of Black River Bridge
Q.3. tobacco in 1860
Q.4. Asia Minor under the Greeks and Romans

CHAPTER FIVE

Q.2. the Saint Louis Missouri Fur Company
Q.3. the economy of expanding Europe in the
     sixteenth and seventeenth centuries
     colonial settlement
Q.4. 1648-1688
     the social foundations of state power

CHAPTER SIX

Q.2. Hedvig Charlotta Nordenflycht
Q.3. Thomas Mun
Q.4. Benjamin Barker Odell
Q.5. William Curtis Nunn

CHAPTER SEVEN

Q.3. European diplomatic history
     the diplomatic history of World War I
Q.4. Bohemian immigration to Wisconsin
Q.5. urbanization in Ghana
     1972

CHAPTER EIGHT

Q.2. India
     1975
Q.3. the history of education
     education in Africa
Q.4. Thirty Years' War
     1965-69

CHAPTER NINE

Q.2. Journal of American History
     vol. 55, no. 1, June 1968
     a. "The Convergence of Moods and the Cuban-
        Bond 'Conspiracy' of 1898"
     b. Thomas A. Bailey
     c. This article is an expanded version of
        an address presented to what
        organization on April 18, 1968
     d. California Ranchos and Farms, 1846-1862.
Q.3. Ohio

CHAPTER TEN

Q.2. Democrats and Progressives: The 1948
     Presidential Election as a Test of
     Postwar Liberalism
     Allen Yarnell
Q.3. Negro Slavery in Latin America
     Rolando Mellafe
     v. 4, no. 6, April 1976
Q.4. Uncertain Friendship: American-French
     Diplomatic Relations Through the Cold
     War
     Marvin R. Zahniser
     v. 4, no. 3, September 1976

CHAPTER ELEVEN

Q.2. Glenwood City
Q.3. Tunisia
     1971
Q.4. a. September-October 1968

CHAPTER TWELVE

Q.2. Alaska
     1974
Q.3. Kansas
Q.4. the Siegfried Line campaign

MATERIALS & METHODS
FOR
HISTORY RESEARCH

Fill-ins by Book

Book No. ___14___

CHAPTER ONE

Q.2. an introductory political science course
Q.3. an occupational biographical source with
        coverage limited to the British
        parliament
Q.4. the Roman Republic and Empire
        constitutional and legal history
Q.5. World War II
        the military history of the conflict

CHAPTER TWO

Q.2. 1953
Q.3. Mar. 2, 1887
Q.4. World War I
        a. What was the subject of the first
            "group" of Japan's 21 Demands accepted
            by China in 1915

CHAPTER THREE

Q.2. The Sudan
Q.3. a. Pennsylvania
Q.4. African
        a. Nigeria
        (Use the 1975 edition.)
Q.5. Mar. 22, 1976
Q.6. Romford

CHAPTER FOUR

Q.2. Battle of Blandensburg
Q.3. tobacco in 1890
Q.4. Italy to 218 B.C.

CHAPTER FIVE

Q.2. the Spoils System
Q.3. the economy of expanding Europe in the
        sixteenth and seventeenth centuries
        transport and trade routes
Q.4. 1648-1688
        French Diplomacy and Foreign Policy in
            their European setting

CHAPTER SIX

Q.2. Józef Pilsudski
Q.3. Marchamont Needham
Q.4. Herbert Levi Osgood
Q.5. Lawrence Jay Oliva

CHAPTER SEVEN

Q.3. European diplomatic history
        territorial questions during World War I
Q.4. land companies in Virginia
Q.5. revolutions and revolutionary movements in
        Tanzania
        1972

CHAPTER EIGHT

Q.2. Japan
        1975
Q.3. the history of education
        education in Latin America
Q.4. Battle of Waterloo
        1975

CHAPTER NINE

Q.2. Journal of American History
        vol. 56, no. 1, June 1969
        a. "Wendell Phillips and American
            Institutions"
        b. C. Vann Woodward
        c. When and where was this paper delivered
            as the presidential address of the
            Organization of American Historians
        d. Melodrama Unveiled: American Theater and
            Culture, 1800-1850
Q.3. Oregon

CHAPTER TEN

Q.2. The Secessionist Impulse: Alabama and
        Mississipi in 1860
        William Barney
Q.3. A Yankee Guerrillero: Frederick Funsto and
        the Cuban Insurrection 1896-1897
        Thomas W. Crouch
        v. 4, no. 7, May/June 1976
Q.4. Eagle and the Sword: The Federalists and
        the Creation of the Military
        Establishment in America, 1783-1802
        Richard H. Kohn
        v. 4, no. 1, March 1976

CHAPTER ELEVEN

Q.2. Arcadia
Q.3. Sierra Leone
        1971
Q.4. a. July-September 1973

CHAPTER TWELVE

Q.2. Maryland
        1974
Q.3. Kentucky
Q.4. the German campaigns in the Northern
        Theater of operations, 1940-1945

MATERIALS & METHODS
FOR
HISTORY RESEARCH

Fill-ins by Book

Book No. 15

CHAPTER ONE

Q.2. a Canadian literature survey course
Q.3. an historical atlas with coverage limited
     to United States military history
Q.4. the Roman Republic and Empire
     cultural developments, specifically on
     religion
Q.5. World War II
     the development of atomic weaponry

CHAPTER TWO

Q.2. 1954
Q.3. Mar. 1, 1913
Q.4. early nineteenth century diplomacy
     a. What was the name of the treaty agreed
        upon by the Austrians after the Battle
        of Wagram

CHAPTER THREE

Q.2. Upper Volta
Q.3. a. South Carolina
Q.4. Latin American
     a. Paraguay
     (Use the 1975 edition.)
Q.5. Apr. 6, 1976
Q.6. Shipley

CHAPTER FOUR

Q.2. Battle of Buell-Comanche (1875)
Q.3. tobacco in 1920
Q.4. Greece at the time of the War with Persia

CHAPTER FIVE

Q.2. the Oneida Colony
Q.3. the economy of expanding Europe in the
     sixteenth and seventeenth centuries
     crops and livestock
Q.4. 1793-1830
     the emancipation of Latin America

CHAPTER SIX

Q.2. Rasmus Christian Rask
Q.3. William Pierrepont
Q.4. Dean Richmond
Q.5. Frank Ross Peterson

CHAPTER SEVEN

Q.3. the history of Great Britain
     Ireland and World War I
Q.4. the Adams-Onis Treaty between Texas and
     Oklahoma
Q.5. urbanization in Uganda
     1972

CHAPTER EIGHT

Q.2. Latin America
     1975
Q.3. the history of political theory
     the career and writings of Montesquieu
Q.4. Battle of the Nile
     1965-69

CHAPTER NINE

Q.2. Journal of American History
     vol. 57, no. 1, June 1970
     a. "France and the War of 1812"
     b. Humbert S. Nelli
     c. In what year did the J. T. Salter book
        Boss Rule appear
     d. The Democratic Republic, 1801-1815
Q.3. Pennsylvania

CHAPTER TEN

Q.2. A Matter of Allegiance: Maryland from 1850-
     1861
     William J. Evitts
Q.3. Race, Class, and Politics in Colonial
     Mexico, 1610-1670
     J. I. Israel
     v. 3, no. 10, September 1975
Q.4. Men and Wealth in the United States 1850-
     1870
     Lee Soltow
     v. 4, no. 2, June 1976

CHAPTER ELEVEN

Q.2. Kewaunee
Q.3. Dahomey
     1971
Q.4. July-September 1972

CHAPTER TWELVE

Q.2. Nevada
     1974
Q.3. Louisiana
Q.4. the effects of the climate on the Russian
     Campaign

MATERIALS & METHODS
FOR
HISTORY RESEARCH

Fill-ins by Book

Book No. __16__

CHAPTER ONE

Q.2. a French literature survey course
Q.3. an historical atlas with coverage limited
   to the classical world
Q.4. the Roman Republic and Empire
   social and/or economic developments
Q.5. domestic developments since 1945
   the Truman administration

CHAPTER TWO

Q.2. 1955
Q.3. July 1, 1898
Q.4. post World War II German history
   a. Who was the Minister for Foreign Affairs
      appointed by Kurt Kiesinger in 1966

CHAPTER THREE

Q.2. Uruguay
Q.3. a. Tennessee
Q.4. European
   a. Spain
   (Use the 1975 edition.)
Q.5. Apr. 27, 1976
Q.6. Stretford

CHAPTER FOUR

Q.2. Battle of Canyon Creek
Q.3. tobacco in 1950
Q.4. the Athenian Empire (450 B.C.)

CHAPTER FIVE

Q.2. the Pious Fund Controversy
Q.3. the economy of expanding Europe in the
   sixteenth and seventeenth centuries
   European economic institutions
Q.4. 1763-1793
   the breakdown of the old régime in France

CHAPTER SIX

Q.2. George Sand
Q.3. Thomas Pride
Q.4. Stephen Sayre
Q.5. Herbert Harvey Rowen

CHAPTER SEVEN

Q.3. American frontier history
   the Pony Express
Q.4. Chinese immigrants in Nevada
Q.5. socialism in Zambia
   1971

CHAPTER EIGHT

Q.2. Russia
   1975
Q.3. recent American history
   the careers and writing of Reinhold Niebuhr
Q.4. Battle of Hastings
   1965-69

CHAPTER NINE

Q.2. Journal of American History
   vol. 57, no. 3, December 1970
   a. "Urban Crime and Criminal Justice: The
      Chicago Case"
   b. Mary R. Kihl
   c. Who was the British ambassador mentioned
      in the article
   d. Cornwallis: The American Adventure
Q.3. Rhode Island

CHAPTER TEN

Q.2. Nor is It Over Yet: Florida in the Era of
   Reconstruction, 1863-1877
   Jerrell H. Shofner
Q.3. Har Dayal: Hindu Revolutionary and
   Rationalist
   Emily C. Brown
   v. 4, no. 1, October 1975
Q.4. The French Navy and American Independence
   A Study of Arms and Diplomacy, 1774-1787
   Jonathan R. Dull
   v. 4, no. 3, September 1976

CHAPTER ELEVEN

Q.2. Bayfield
Q.3. Mali
   1971
Q.4. a. April-June 1972

CHAPTER TWELVE

Q.2. North Carolina
   1972
Q.3. Maine
Q.4. Salerna to Cassino: the Mediterranean
   Theater of operations

MATERIALS & METHODS
FOR
HISTORY RESEARCH

Fill-ins by Book

Book No. ___17___

CHAPTER ONE

Q.2. an introductory biological sciences course
Q.3. an historical atlas with coverage limited
     to the medieval world
Q.4. the Roman Republic and Empire
     cultural developments, specifically
     literature
Q.5. domestic developments since 1945
     the Eisenhower administration

CHAPTER TWO

Q.2. 1956
Q.3. June 1, 1898
Q.4. post World War II Russian history
     a. Who was the man Andrei Gromyko replaced
        as Russian Foreign Minister

CHAPTER THREE

Q.2. Turkey
Q.3. a. Utah
Q.4. African
     a. Sudan
     (Use the 1975 edition.)
Q.5. May 11, 1976
Q.6. Tiverton

CHAPTER FOUR

Q.2. Battle of Carnifex Ferry
Q.3. wheat in 1840
Q.4. Greece at the beginning of the
     Peloponnesian War

CHAPTER FIVE

Q.2. the Walla Walla Settlements
Q.3. the Industrial Revolution
     transportation
Q.4. 1898-1945
     the diplomatic history of the Second
     World War

CHAPTER SIX

Q.2. Gabriel Tarde
Q.3. Thomas Roe
Q.4. William Miskey Singerly
Q.5. John L. Shover

CHAPTER SEVEN

Q.3. Europe in the twentieth century
     Fascism in Italy
Q.4. the settlement of Arapaho Indians in
     Oklahoma
Q.5. urbanization in Tanzania
     1971

CHAPTER EIGHT

Q.2. Turkey
     1975
Q.3. colonial American history
     the career of William Penn
Q.4. Battle of Hastings
     1975

CHAPTER NINE

Q.2. Journal of American History
     vol. 58, no. 1, June 1971
     a. "Woodrow Wilson and the Mexican
        Interventionist Movement of 1919"
     b. Stanley E. Hilton
     c. In what year did the cited book by
        Langer and Gleason (The Challenge to
        Isolation) appear
     d. A Financial History of the United States
Q.3. Texas

CHAPTER TEN

Q.2. Louisiana Reconstructed, 1863-1877
     Joe Gray Taylor
Q.3. The Forgotten Sioux: An Ethnohistory of the
        Lower Brule Reservation
     Ernest L. Schusky
     v. 4, no. 2, Nov./Dec. 1975
Q.4. Water and the West: The Colorado River
        Compact and the Politics of Water in the
        American West
     Norris Hundley, Jr.
     v. 4, no. 2, June 1976

CHAPTER ELEVEN

Q.2. Brodhead
Q.3. Zambia
     1971
Q.4. a. April-June 1975

CHAPTER TWELVE

Q.2. Texas
     1974
Q.3. Massachusetts
Q.4. interservice relations in the Pacific
     command

MATERIALS & METHODS
FOR
HISTORY RESEARCH

Fill-ins by Book

Book No. __18__

CHAPTER ONE

Q.2. a Russian literature survey course
Q.3. an index to a major American newspaper
Q.4. Ancient Greece and the Hellenistic World
political institutions, specifically the
Greek city states
Q.5. domestic developments since 1945
the Kennedy administration

CHAPTER TWO

Q.2. 1957
Q.3. Feb. 11, 1903
Q.4. post World War II Russian history
a. What was the name of Yuri Gagarin's
spacecraft

CHAPTER THREE

Q.2. Togo
Q.3. a. Virginia
Q.4. African
a. Togo
(Use the 1975 edition.)
Q.5. Apr. 8, 1976
Q.6. Whitehaven

CHAPTER FOUR

Q.2. Battle of Wisconsin Heights
Q.3. wheat in 1860
Q.4. Greece under Theban Headship

CHAPTER FIVE

Q.2. the Wisconsin Idea
Q.3. the Industrial Revolution
the opening up of new territories
Q.4. 1898-1945
the Peace Settlement of Versailles

CHAPTER SIX

Q.2. José Francisco Uriburu
Q.3. Philip Skippon
Q.4. Reuben Gold Thwaites
Q.5. Frederick Barnes Tolles

CHAPTER SEVEN

Q.3. Modern European diplomatic history
Italian invasion of Ethiopia
Q.4. removal of the Wyandot Indians from Ohio
Q.5. revolutions and revolutionary movements in
Kenya
1971

CHAPTER EIGHT

Q.2. Asia
1974
Q.3. recent cultural history
the career and writings of Gertrude Stein
Q.4. Battle of the Marne
1970-74

CHAPTER NINE

Q.2. Journal of American History
vol. 58, no. 3, December 1971
a. "The Texas Supreme Court and Trial
Rights of Blacks, 1845-1860"
b. Harvard Sitkoff
c. In what year did the cited book by
Herbert Garfinkel (When Negroes March)
appear
d. Free Soil: The Election of 1848
Q.3. Vermont

CHAPTER TEN

Q.2. Space, Time and Freedom: The Quest for
Nationality and the Irrepressible
Conflict, 1815-1861
Major L. Wilson
Q.3. The American Revolution and the West Indies
Charles W. Toth
v. 4, no. 3, January 1976
Q.4. The Making of the Monroe Doctrine
Ernest R. May
v. 4, no. 3, September 1976

CHAPTER ELEVEN

Q.2. Palmyra
Q.3. Zaire
1971
Q.4. a. October-December 1974

CHAPTER TWELVE

Q.2. Maine
1974
Q.3. Minnesota
Q.4. the Bougainville and Northern Solomons
Campaign

MATERIALS & METHODS
FOR
HISTORY RESEARCH

Fill-ins by Book

Book No. __19__

CHAPTER ONE

Q.2. a Spanish literature survey course
Q.3. a regional biographical source with
     coverage limited to Latin America
Q.4. Ancient Greece and the Hellenistic World
     economic history, specifically the
     development of agriculture
Q.5. foreign relations since 1945
     the cold war

CHAPTER TWO

Q.2. 1958
Q.3. June 3, 1916
Q.4. Marxism
     a. What were the dates of the Second
        International Workingmen's Association

CHAPTER THREE

Q.2. Thailand
Q.3. a. West Virginia
Q.4. European
     a. Sweden
     (Use the 1975 edition.)
Q.5. May 1, 1976
Q.6. Woking

CHAPTER FOUR

Q.2. Battle of Wood Lake
Q.3. wheat in 1890
Q.4. Asia Minor after the treaty of Apamea

CHAPTER FIVE

Q.2. the Lafayette Escadrille
Q.3. the Industrial Revolution
     agrarian policies and industrialization in
     Russia
Q.4. 1870-1898
     the partition of Africa

CHAPTER SIX

Q.2. Georg Weber
Q.3. Thomas Sydenham
Q.4. Israel Washburn
Q.5. Paul Albert Varg

CHAPTER SEVEN

Q.3. the history of France
     the Restoration Period (1814-1830)
Q.4. the railroad and settlement patterns in
     Minnesota
Q.5. economic growth and development in Tunisia
     1971

CHAPTER EIGHT

Q.2. Brazil
     1974
Q.3. the history of economic theory
     the career and writings of David Ricardo
Q.4. Battle of New Orleans
     1965-69

CHAPTER NINE

Q.2. Journal of American History
     vol. 59, no. 3, December 1972
     a. "The Washington Administration's
        Decision to Crush the Whiskey
        Rebellion"
     b. Christopher G. Wye
     c. What 1971 award did this essay win
     d. Iowa on the Eve of the Civil War: A
        Decade of Frontier Politics
Q.3. Virginia

CHAPTER TEN

Q.2. The American Revolution of 1800
     Daniel Sisson
Q.3. The National Archives and Urban Research
     Jerome Finster
     v. 3, no. 5, March 1975
Q.4. Polish-American Politics in Chicago, 1888-
     1940
     Edward R. Kantowicz
     v. 4, no. 1, March 1976

CHAPTER ELEVEN

Q.2. Crandon
Q.3. Zambia
     1970
Q.4. a. July-September 1976

CHAPTER TWELVE

Q.2. Washington
     1972
Q.3. Mississippi
Q.4. PT boat operations in the U. S. Navy

MATERIALS & METHODS
FOR
HISTORY RESEARCH

Fill-ins by Book

Book No.   20

CHAPTER ONE

Q.2. an introductory physics course
Q.3. a world gazetteer
Q.4. Ancient Greece and the Hellenistic World
        military history
Q.5. foreign relations since 1945
        the Vietnam war

CHAPTER TWO

Q.2. 1959
Q.3. May 30, 1908
Q.4. Marxism
        a. What were the publication years of the
            three volumes of Marx's Das Kapital

CHAPTER THREE

Q.2. Syria
Q.3. Wyoming
Q.4. African
        a. Zambia
        (Use the 1975 edition.)
Q.5. May 4, 1976
Q.6. Worthing

CHAPTER FOUR

Q.2. Battle of Wounded Knee
Q.3. wheat in 1920
Q.4. Asia Minor before Mithradatic Wars

CHAPTER FIVE

Q.2. the Mecklenburg Declaration of Independence
Q.3. the Industrial Revolution
        technological change and development in
            Western Europe
Q.4. 1870-1898
        political rivalries in the Mediterranean
        the Middle East and Egypt

CHAPTER SIX

Q.2. Arthur Zimmermann
Q.3. John Wildman
Q.4. Joseph Albert Wright
Q.5. Mack Walker

CHAPTER SEVEN

Q.3. ancient history
        the Persian Wars (500-449 B.C.)
Q.4. the Abnaki Indians in Maine
Q.5. revolutions and revolutionary movements in
        the Congro Republic (Brazzaville)

CHAPTER EIGHT

Q.2. Cuba
        1974
Q.3. the history of British imperialism
        the career of Cecil Rhodes
Q.4. Battle of New Orleans
        1970-74

CHAPTER NINE

Q.2. Journal of American History
        vol. 60, no. 3, December 1973
        a. "The Transformation of Urban Politics
            1700-1765"
        b. John D. Baker
        c. In what year did the cited book by
            Richard Lowitt (George W. Norris)
            appear
        d. Flood Tide of Empire: Spain and the
            Pacific Northwest, 1543-1819
Q.3. New York

CHAPTER TEN

Q.2. The New Country: A Social History of the
        American Frontier, 1776-1890
        Richard A. Bartlett
Q.3. A Most Unique Machine: The Michigan Origins
        of the American Automobile Industry
        George S. May
        v. 3, no. 7, May/June 1975
Q.4. The Impending Crisis, 1848-1861
        David M. Potter
        v. 4, no. 4, December 1976

CHAPTER ELEVEN

Q.2. Kaukauna
Q.3. Tunisia
        1970
Q.4. a. November-December 1967

CHAPTER TWELVE

Q.2. Michigan
        1974
Q.3. New Hampshire
Q.4. the Imperial Japanese Navy

8
Answer Sheets

Because the student assignment pages are an integral part of the workbook, the most convenient way to proceed is to have students turn in the entire workbook periodically for the evaluation of assigned work. At any given time, therefore, the instructor is likely to have in hand a number of workbooks with more than one completed assignment to correct. To facilitate grading, the answer sheets are arranged by complete book. The answers provided on the answer sheet appear as they appear in the source. No answer has been written for the first question in each chapter, because it is possible for students to provide different yet correct answers. Also, it provides the instructor with a means for determining whether each student has an adequate overall understanding of the type of source under discussion.

Although the answers provided on the following pages have been carefully checked and tested, students may interpret the questions differently, or through means not previously used by any other student, uncover a different and yet correct answer. These possibilities should be kept in mind by the instructor while grading the assignments.

MATERIALS & METHODS
FOR
HISTORY RESEARCH

Answer by Book

Book No.   1

CHAPTER ONE

Q.2. a. Bibliographical guide to the study of
          the literature of the U.S.A.
      b. Guide to Reference Books, p. 315

Q.3. a. A Guide to the Study of Medieval History
      b. The Historian's Handbook: A Descriptive
          Guide to Reference Works, p. 40.

Q.4. a. Feudalism
      b. Guide to Historical Literature, p. 184

Q.5. a. Economic Origins of Jeffersonian
          Democracy
      b. Harvard Guide to American History,
          p. 780

CHAPTER TWO

Q.2. a. $42,967,531 (in $1,000)
      b. Historical Statistics of the United
          States; Colonial Times to 1970,
          p. 1117

Q.3. a. Shipping Act
      b. Encyclopedia of American History, p. 329

Q.4. a. Great Britain, France, Germany, Italy,
          Australia, Spain, Netherlands, Russia,
          Turkey
      b. Encyclopedia of World History, p. 869

CHAPTER THREE

Q.2. a. Manuel Trucco
          1736 Massachusetts Avenue, NW,
          Washington, D.C. 20036
      b. Statesman's Yearbook; Statistical and
          Historical Annual of the States of the
          World, p. 826

Q.3. a. $820 million
      b. Statistical Abstract of the United
          States, p. 263

Q.4. a. 126 452; 60 116 (million Cruzeiros)
      b. Statistical Yearbook, p. 707

Q.5. a. Wallace enters Presidential Race
      b. World Almanac, p. 912

Q.6. a. I. L. Evans, Labour
      b. Whitaker's Almanack, p. 322

CHAPTER FOUR

Q.2. a. Plate 61, Proclamation Line of 1763,
          Indian Cessions and the Land Companies
      b. Atlas of American History

Q.3. a. Historical Atlas of the United States
      b. Map no. 101, p. 69

Q.4. a. Historical Atlas
      b. p. 1, 1:2,000,000

CHAPTER FIVE

Q.2. a. Dictionary of American History, v. 7,
          p. 64
      b. The Puritan Republic

Q.3. a. Charles Parain
      b. Cambridge Economic History of Europe,
          pp. 761-765

Q.4. a. J. O. Lindsay
      b. Peace settlement, 1713-14
      c. New Cambridge Modern History, v. 7

CHAPTER SIX

Q.2. a. France, 1560-1619
      b. Webster's Biographical Dictionary, p. 64

Q.3. a. physician
      b. Dictionary of National Biography, v. 1,
          p. 39

Q.4. a. Men of Mark in Ga.
      b. Dictionary of American Biography, v. 1,
          p. 412

Q.5. a. U. of California, Los Angeles
      b. Directory of American Scholars, p. 5

CHAPTER SEVEN

Q.3. a. Corinth: the story of a contraband camp.
          C. Walker. Civil War History 20:5-22
          Mr '74.
      b. p. 487

Q.4. a. Norwood, Frederick A. "Strangers in a
          Strange Land: Removal of the Wyandot
          Indians." Methodist Hist., 1975,
          13(3): 45-60
      b. America: History and Life, p. 182

Q.5. a. Kuper, Leo. "Race, Class and Power:
          Some Comments on Revolutionary Change."
          Comparative Studies in Soc. and Hist.,
          1972, 14(4): 400-421.
      b. p. 31

CHAPTER EIGHT

Q.2. a. Stookey, Robert W. America and the Arab
        states; an uneasy encounter.
     b. Bibliographic Index, p. 23 or 490

Q.3. a. Joseph Guerin Fucilla and Joseph Medard
        Carriere. D'Annunzio abroad. A
        bibliographical essay.
     b. A World Bibliography of Bibliographies
        and of Bibliographical Catalogs,
        Calendars, Abstracts, Digests, Indexes
        and the Like, v. 1, c. 395

Q.4. a. Nicolas, Nicolas Harris. History of the
        battle of Agincourt. London, Muller,
        1970.
     b. Subject Catalog; A Cumulative List of
        Works Represented by Library of
        Congress Printed Cards, v. 2, p. 109

CHAPTER NINE

Q.2. a. Lenore O'Boyle, Connecticut College
     b. "Winston Churchill versus the Webbs: The
        Origins of British Unemployment
        Insurance"
     c. National Insurance Act of 1911
     d. Stanley Spector

Q.3. a. Alabama Review; a journal of Alabama
        history
     b. Magazines for Libraries, p. 416

CHAPTER TEN

Q.2. a. Journal of American History, 62:161-2,
        June 1975, C. W. Grantham.
     b. p. 885

Q.3. a. William H. Pease
     b. University of Maine at Orono
     c. pp. 225-226

Q.4. a. Richard Buel, Jr.
     b. Wesleyan University
     c. pp. 378-382

CHAPTER ELEVEN

Q.2. a. Record-Herald
     b. 1873
     c. p. 897

Q.3. a. Pres. Pompidou arrives, Niamey, Niger,
        for official visit
     b. Ja 25,32:5
     c. p. 1549

Q.4. a. Administration--consultative document
        issued
     b. May 18, 2a
     c. p. 100

CHAPTER TWELVE

Q.2. a. Historic Preservation Commission.
        Historic resources inventory, 1974,
        compiled and written by Earle G.
        Shettleworth, Jr. (Augusta, 1974)
        128 l. illus.
     b. Monthly Checklist of State Publications,
        p. 720

Q.3. a. Alaska. Division of State Libraries.
        State publications received. [1965+]
        Juneau. [annual]
     b. Government Publications: A Guide to
        Bibliographical Tools, p. 88

Q.4. a. (54) 8846
     b. United States Army in World War II:
        European theater of operations,
        Supreme Command. 1954. xxi+607 p.

MATERIALS & METHODS
FOR
HISTORY RESEARCH

Answer by Book

Book No. __2__

CHAPTER ONE

Q.2. a. The student anthropologist's handbook;
        a guide to research, training, and
        career
     b. Guide to Reference Books, p. 467

Q.3. a. Bibliography of British History
     b. The Historian's Handbook: A Descriptive
        Guide to Reference Works, p. 43

Q.4. a. French chivalry: chivalric ideas and
        practices in mediaeval France
     b. Guide to Historical Literature, p. 185

Q.5. a. Whiskey Rebels
     b. Harvard Guide to American History,
        p. 783

CHAPTER TWO

Q.2. a. $48,961,444 (in $1,000)
     b. Historical Statistics of the United
        States; Colonial Times to 1970,
        p. 1117

Q.3. a. Hay-Bunau-Varilla Treaty
     b. Encyclopedia of American History,
        p. 349

Q.4. a. General Erich Ludendorff
     b. Encyclopedia of World History, p. 1006

CHAPTER THREE

Q.2. a. Julio Cesar Turbay-Ayala
        2118 Leroy Pl., NW,
        Washington, D.C. 20008
     b. Statesman's Yearbook; Statistical and
        Historical Annual of the States of the
        World, p. 849

Q.3. a. $260 million
     b. Statistical Abstract of the United
        States, p. 263

Q.4. a. 14.29; 9.36 (000 million CFA francs)
     b. Statistical Yearbook, p. 707

Q.5. a. Reagan to seek Republican Nomination
     b. World Almanac, p. 912

Q.6. a. I. S. M. MacCormick, Scottish
        Nationalist
     b. Whitaker's Almanack, p. 322

CHAPTER FOUR

Q.2. a. Plate 130, Trans-Mississippi, 1861-1865
     b. Atlas of American History

Q.3. a. Historical Atlas of the United States
     b. Map no. 102, p. 69

Q.4. a. Historical Atlas
     b. p. 4, 1:10,000,000

CHAPTER FIVE

Q.2. a. Dictionary of American History, v. 6,
        p. 138
     b. Thomas Ritchie: A Study in Virginia
        Politics

Q.3. a. Richard Koebner
     b. Cambridge Economic History of Europe,
        pp. 745-755

Q.4. a. Albert Richardson
     b. Art and literature theoretically
        classical and derivative
     c. New Cambridge Modern History, v. 7

CHAPTER SIX

Q.2. a. Italy, 1896-1940
     b. Webster's Biographical Dictionary, p. 92

Q.3. a. diplomatist and scholar
     b. Dictionary of National Biography, v. 2,
        p. 756 or v. 5, p. 294

Q.4. a. Henry W. Bellows: His Life and Character
     b. Dictionary of American Biography, v. 2,
        p. 169

Q.5. a. Columbia U.
     b. Directory of American Scholars, p. 27

CHAPTER SEVEN

Q.3. a. Cold war revisionism and the origins of
        the Korean conflict: the Kolko thesis.
        W. Stueck. Pacific Historical Review
        42:537-75 N '73.
     b. p. 245

Q.4. a. Kousser, J. Morgan. "A Black Protest in
        the 'Era of Accommodation'." Arkansas
        Hist. Q., 1975, 34(2): 149-178.
     b. America: History and Life, p. 419

Q.5. a. Okafor, Nduka. "Higher Education in
        Pre-Independence Nigerian Politics."
        Nigeria Mag., 1971 (107-109): 72-76.
     b. p. 157

CHAPTER EIGHT

Q.2. a. Hinton, Harold C. Three and a half
          powers; the new balance in Asia.
     b. Bibliographic Index, p. 31 or 490

Q.3. a. Frederick Albert Pottle. The literary
          career of James Boswell, esq., being
          the bibliographical materials for a
          life of Boswell.
     b. A World Bibliography of Bibliographies
        and of Bibliographical Catalogs,
        Calendars, Abstracts, Digests, Indexes
        and the Like, v. 1, c. 938

Q.4. a. The Boke of noblesse: addressed to King
          Edward the Fourth on his invasion of
          France in 1475. With an introduction
          by John Gough Nichols. New York,
          B. Franklin, 1972.
     b. Subject Catalog; A Cumulative List of
        Works Represented by Library of
        Congress Printed Cards, v. 42, p. 532

CHAPTER NINE

Q.2. a. Nels Bailkey, Tulane University
     b. "The 'New Left' and American History:
        Some Recent Trends in United States
        Historiography"
     c. 1959
     d. David Owen

Q.3. a. The Alaska Journal; history and arts of
          the north-quarterly
     b. Magazines for Libraries, p. 416

CHAPTER TEN

Q.2. a. Journal of American History, 62:170-1,
          June 1975, A. Rolle.
     b. p. 853

Q.3. a. Werner Braatz
     b. University of Wisconsin-Oshkosh
     c. p. 205

Q.4. a. John W. Coffey
     b. Stanford University
     c. pp. 546-552

CHAPTER ELEVEN

Q.2. a. Gazette
     b. 1845
     c. p. 903

Q.3. a. Nigeria's '71 econ rev (Econ Survey of
          Africa); '72 econ forecast sees oil
          indus, which is expected to yield Govt
          revenue of close to $1-billion in '72,
          as key factor; Nigerian workers illus
     b. Ja 31,44:5
     c. p. 1549

Q.4. a. Abuse of--medical union leader calls for
          public inquiry
     b. Mar. 30, 3g
     c. p. 142

CHAPTER TWELVE

Q.2. a. Division of State Parks, Outdoor
        Recreation and Historic Sites.
        Historic preservation annual report.
        1973. (Honolulu) 41 p. illus.
     b. Monthly Checklist of State Publications,
        p. 98

Q.3. a. Arkansas. University. Library.
        Checklist of Arkansas state
        publications received by the
        University of Arkansas Library.
        no. 1+ 1943+ Fayetteville, 1944+
        semiannual.
     b. Government Publications: A Guide to
        Bibliographical Tools, p. 90

Q.4. a. (54) 16187
     b. German antiguerrilla operations in
        Balkans (1941-1944). August 1954.
        vi+82 p.

MATERIALS & METHODS
FOR
HISTORY RESEARCH

Answer by Book

Book No. 3

CHAPTER ONE

Q.2. a. Astronomy and astrophysics; a
        bibliographical guide
     b. Guide to Reference Books, p. 714

Q.3. a. Oriental and Asian Bibliography: An
        Introduction with Some Reference to
        Africa
     b. The Historian's Handbook: A Descriptive
        Guide to Reference Works, pp. 52-53

Q.4. a. A history of the crusades
     b. Guide to Historical Literature, p. 186

Q.5. a. Social Ideas of Northern Evangelists,
        1826-1860
     b. Harvard Guide to American History,
        p. 805

CHAPTER TWO

Q.2. a. $72,422,445 (in $1,000)
     b. Historical Statistics of the United
        States; Colonial Times to 1970,
        p. 1117

Q.3. a. Amistad Case
     b. Encyclopedia of American History, p. 219

Q.4. a. National Socialists, Nationalists,
        Catholic Center Party
     b. Encyclopedia of World History, p. 1009

CHAPTER THREE

Q.2. a. Francisco Bertrand Galindo
        2308 California St., NW,
        Washington, D.C. 20008
     b. Statesman's Yearbook; Statistical and
        Historical Annual of the States of the
        World, p. 905

Q.3. a. $511 million
     b. Statistical Abstract of the United
        States, p. 263

Q.4. a. 837; 1 004 (000 million Escudos)
     b. Statistical Yearbook, p. 707

Q.5. a. Byrd Enters Democratic Race, Sanford
        quits
     b. World Almanac, p. 917

Q.6. a. D. B. Mitchell, Conservative
     b. Whitaker's Almanack, p. 323

CHAPTER FOUR

Q.2. a. Plate 111, Wisconsin, Iowa and Minnesota
        Territories, 1832-1858
     b. Atlas of American History

Q.3. a. Historical Atlas of the United States
     b. Map no. 217, p. 143

Q.4. a. Historical Atlas
     b. p. 5, 1:20,000,000

CHAPTER FIVE

Q.2. a. Dictionary of American History, v. 5,
        p. 227
     b. The Crisis of 1830-1842 in Canadian-
        American Relations

Q.3. a. Marc Bloch
     b. Cambridge Economic History of Europe,
        pp. 780-789

Q.4. a. E. A. Beller
     b. The religious controversies of the Holy
        Roman Empire
     c. New Cambridge Modern History, v. 4

CHAPTER SIX

Q.2. a. Peru, 1832-1905
     b. Webster's Biographical Dictionary,
        p. 231

Q.3. a. author
     b. Dictionary of National Biography, v. 3,
        p. 275 or v. 7, p. 275

Q.4. a. Men of Mark in Va.
     b. Dictionary of American Biography, v. 3,
        pp. 439-40

Q.5. a. Stanford U.
     b. Directory of American Scholars, p. 111

CHAPTER SEVEN

Q.3. a. Philipp Melanchthon (1497-1560) Wilhelm
        Zimmerman (1807-1878) and the dilemma
        of Muntzer historiography. A. Friesen.
        Church History 43:164-182 Je '74.
     b. p. 342

Q.4. a. Garr, Daniel. "Planning, Politics and
        Plunder: The Missions and Indian
        Pueblos of Hispanic California."
        Southern California Q., 1972, 54(4):
        291-312.
     b. America: History and Life, p. 162

CHAPTER SEVEN, continued

Q.5. a. Welch, Claude E. "Praetorianism in
          Commonwealth West Africa." J. of
          Modern African Studies [Great Britain],
          1972, 10(2): 203-222.
     b. p. 39

CHAPTER EIGHT

Q.2. a. Moore, John Hammond, ed. American
          alliance; Australia, New Zealand and
          the U.S.: 1940-1970.
     b. Bibliographic Index, p. 35 or 490

Q.3. a. Francesco Cordasco. Edmund Burke: a
          handlist of critical notices and
          studies.
     b. A World Bibliography of Bibliographies
        and of Bibliographical Catalogs,
        Calendars, Abstracts, Digests, Indexes
        and the Like, v. 1, c. 1062

Q.4. a. Williams, Daniel Thomas. The battle of
          Bosworth, 22 August 1485. Leicester,
          Leicester University Press, 1973.
     b. Subject Catalog; A Cumulative List of
        Works Represented by Library of
        Congress Printed Cards, v. 10, p. 456

CHAPTER NINE

Q.2. a. David B. Tyack, University of Illinois
     b. "The Moriscos: An Ottoman Fifth Column
        in Sixteenth-Century Spain"
     c. Americo Castro
     d. Martin Ridge

Q.3. a. Illinois History; a magazine for young
          people or Illinois State Historical
          Society. Journal.
     b. Magazines for Libraries, p. 417 or
          p. 418

CHAPTER TEN

Q.2. a. Journal of American History, 62:187-9,
          June 1975, R. Lowitt.
     b. p. 907

Q.3. a. Rodger Yeager
     b. West Virginia University
     c. pp. 170-171

Q.4. a. Robert M. Cover
     b. Yale University
     c. pp. 529-535

CHAPTER ELEVEN

Q.2. a. News-Herald
     b. 1883

     c. p. 907

Q.3. a. Mrs. Nixon arrives, Accra, Ghana, second
          stop in 3-nation African tour;
          greeted by Prime Min Busia; illus
     b. Ja 6,3:3
     c. p. 814

Q.4. a. Administration--Ombudsman to cover
          health service under new act
     b. Nov. 15, 2a
     c. p. 166

CHAPTER TWELVE

Q.2. a. State Dept. of Art, Historical and
          Cultural Preservation. National
          register of historic places. Baton
          Rouge [1975. 2]p.
     b. Monthly Checklist of State Publications,
          p. 448

Q.3. a. California state publications. v. 1+;
          July/Sept. 1947+ Sacremento, Printing
          Division, Documents Section.
     b. Government Publications: A Guide to
        Bibliographical Tools, p. 91

Q.4. a. (68) 9260
     b. Stalingrad to Berlin, the German defeat
        in the East. 1968. xiv+549 p.

MATERIALS & METHODS
FOR
HISTORY RESEARCH

Answer by Book

Book No. __4__

CHAPTER ONE

Q.2. a. The use of economics literature
b. Guide to Reference Books, p. 497

Q.3. a. Encyclopedia of the Social Sciences
b. The Historian's Handbook: A Descriptive
Guide to Reference Works, p. 64

Q.4. a. The growth of papal government in the
Middle Ages: a study in the
ideological relation of clerical to
lay power
b. Guide to Historical Literature, p. 189

Q.5. a. Commerce Clause under Marshall, Taney,
and Waite
b. Harvard Guide to American History,
p. 809

CHAPTER TWO

Q.2. a. $136,696,090 (in $1,000)
b. Historical Statistics of the United
States; Colonial Times to 1970,
p. 1117

Q.3. a. Webster-Ashburton Treaty
b. Encyclopedia of American History, p. 221

Q.4. a. Socialist, Radical Socialist, Communist
b. Encyclopedia of World History, p. 990

CHAPTER THREE

Q.2. a. Julio Asensio-Wunderlich
2220 R St., NW,
Washington, D.C. 20008
b. Statesman's Yearbook; Statistical and
Historical Annual of the States of the
World, p. 1005

Q.3. a. $1,319 million
b. Statistical Abstract of the United
States, p. 263

Q.4. a. 52 866; 30 102 (million Pesos)
b. Statistical Yearbook, p. 707

Q.5. a. Carter Wins in Iowa
b. World Almanac, p. 917

Q.6. a. E. E. Dell, Labour
b. Whitaker's Almanack, p. 324

CHAPTER FOUR

Q.2. a. Plate 114, The Clash with Mexico and
New Boundaries, 1836-1848
b. Atlas of American History

Q.3. a. Historical Atlas of the United States
b. Map no. 218, p. 144

Q.4. a. Historical Atlas
b. pp. 6-7, 1:1,250,000

CHAPTER FIVE

Q.2. a. Dictionary of American History, v. 4,
p. 157
b. John Lind of Minnesota

Q.3. a. Alfons Dopsch
b. Cambridge Economic History of Europe,
pp. 765-774

Q.4. a. M. Roberts
b. Sweden establishes herself as a great
power
c. New Cambridge Modern History, v. 4

CHAPTER SIX

Q.2. a. Hungary, 1803-1876
b. Webster's Biographical Dictionary,
p. 397

Q.3. a. theologian
b. Dictionary of National Biography, v. 4,
p. 252 or v. 10, p. 252

Q.4. a. Frederick Morgan Crunden: A Memorial
Biography
b. Dictionary of American Biography, v. 4,
p. 583

Q.5. a. Princeton
b. Directory of American Scholars, p. 170

CHAPTER SEVEN

Q.3. a. British policy and the Warsaw rising.
F. P. King. Journal of European
Studies 4:1-18 Mr '74.
b. p. 499

Q.4. a. Woods, H. Ted. "The Meredith Family and
the Creek Indian War." North
Louisiana Hist. Assoc. J., 1974, 6(1):
27-29.
b. America: History and Life, p. 336

CHAPTER SEVEN, continued

Q.5. a. Mazrui, Ali A. "The Different Concepts
       of Revolution in East Africa."
       African R. [Tanzania], 1972, 1(4):
       28-51.
    b. p. 33

CHAPTER EIGHT

Q.2. a. Bose, Nemai Sadhan. American attitude
       and policy to the nationalist movement
       in China, 1911-1921.
    b. Bibliographic Index, p. 80 or 490

Q.3. a. Hamilton Bullock Tompkins. Burr
       bibliography.
    b. A World Bibliography of Bibliographies
       and of Bibliographical Catalogs,
       Calendars, Abstracts, Digests, Indexes
       and the Like, v. 1, c 1068

Q.4. a. Young, Peter. Marston Moor, 1644: the
       campaign and the battle. Kineton,
       Roundwood P., 1970.
    b. Subject Catalog; A Cumulative List of
       Works Represented by Library of
       Congress Printed Cards, v. 58, p. 46

CHAPTER NINE

Q.2. a. Gerard E. Silberstein, University of
       Kentucky
    b. "The New Deal and the States"
    c. Jane P. Clark, The Rise of a New
       Federalism (New York, 1938)
    d. Alan R. Schulman

Q.3. a. Annals of Iowa or The Palimpsest
    b. Magazines for Libraries, p. 416 or
       p. 420

CHAPTER TEN

Q.2. a. Historian, 37:523-4, May 1975,
       W. T. Hagan.
    b. p. 871

Q.3. a. Jonathan W. Zophy
    b. Carthage College
    c. pp. 20-21

Q.4. a. Robert C. Twombly
    b. City College, CUNY
    c. pp. 13-18

CHAPTER ELEVEN

Q.2. a. Bulletin
    b. 1875
    c. p. 897

Q.3. a. Easing of pol tensions between Uganda
       and Tanzania, which threatened to
       break up East African Econ Community
       of Kenya, Tanzania and Uganda,
       discussed (Econ Survey of Africa)
    b. Ja 31,54:1
    c. p. 2073

Q.4. a. Expenditure--Parliament discussed
    b. Jan. 29, 7e
    c. p. 150

CHAPTER TWELVE

Q.2. a. Dept. of Natural Resources. Office of
       Land Use. Report of Special
       Environments (Unique Lands)
       Subcommittee. [Lansing] 1974. 79 p.
       illus.
    b. Monthly Checklist of State Publications,
       p. 1022

Q.3. a. Colorado. Division of State Archives
       and Public Records. Checklist [of]
       Colorado publications received. v. 1+
       Oct./Dec. 1964+ Denver. quarterly.
    b. Government Publications: A Guide to
       Bibliographical Tools, p. 93

Q.4. a. (56) 4062
    b. Okinawa, victory in Pacific. 1955.
       viii+332 p.

MATERIALS & METHODS
FOR
HISTORY RESEARCH

Answer by Book

Book No. 5

CHAPTER ONE

Q.2. a. Selective bibliography for the study
        of English and American literature
     b. Guide to Reference Books, p. 322

Q.3. a. Dictionary of American History
     b. The Historian's Handbook: A Descriptive
        Guide to Reference Works, p. 73

Q.4. a. The monastic order in England: a history
        of its development from the times of
        St. Dunstan to the Fourth Lateran
        Council, 943-1216
     b. Guide to Historical Literature, p. 189

Q.5. a. Soil Exhaustion and Civil War
     b. Harvard Guide to American History,
        p. 848

CHAPTER TWO

Q.2. a. $201,003,387 (in $1,000)
     b. Historical Statistics of the United
        States; Colonial Times to 1970,
        p. 1117

Q.3. a. Treaty of Wang Hiya
     b. Encyclopedia of American History, p. 226

Q.4. a. Southeast Asia Collective Defense Treaty
        and Organization (SEATO); French
        defeat in Vietnam
     b. Encyclopedia of World History, p. 1325

CHAPTER THREE

Q.2. a. Habib Bah
        2112 Leroy Pl., NW,
        Washington, D.C. 20008
     b. Statesman's Yearbook; Statistical and
        Historical Annual of the States of
        the World, p. 1007

Q.3. a. $1,179 million
     b. Statistical Abstract of the United
        States, p. 263

Q.4. a. 39.39; 8.81 (000 million Kroner)
     b. Statistical Yearbook, p. 708

Q.5. a. Wallace takes Mississippi
     b. World Almanac, p. 917

Q.6. a. J. Ryman, Labour
     b. Whitaker's Almanack, p. 325

CHAPTER FOUR

Q.2. a. Plate 140, Red River Region, 1865-1885
     b. Atlas of American History

Q.3. a. Historical Atlas of the United States
     b. Map no. 219, p. 144

Q.4. a. Historical Atlas
     b. p. 8, 1:7,500,000

CHAPTER FIVE

Q.2. a. Dictionary of American History
     b. History of Louisiana

Q.3. a. Folke Dovring
     b. Cambridge Economic History of Europe,
        pp. 1007-1011

Q.4. a. G. D. Ramsay
     b. Ferdinand's inheritance and its
        condition
     c. New Cambridge Modern History, v. 3

CHAPTER SIX

Q.2. a. Germany, 1486-1543
     b. Webster's Biographical Dictionary,
        p. 463

Q.3. a. poet
     b. Dictionary of National Biography, v. 5,
        p. 33 or v. 13, p. 33

Q.4. a. Samuel Train Dutton, A Biography
     b. Dictionary of American Biography, v. 5,
        pp. 556-7

Q.5. a. U. of Iowa
     b. Directory of American Scholars, p. 182

CHAPTER SEVEN

Q.3. a. Political recruitment in the Chin
        dynasty. J. S. Tao. American
        Oriental Society Journal 94:24-34
        Ja '74.
     b. p. 74

Q.4. a. Peterson, Charles S. "The Hopis and
        the Mormons, 1858-1873." Utah Hist.
        Q., 1971, 39(2): 179-194.
     b. America: History and Life, p. 6

Q.5. a. Kuper, Leo. "Race, Class and Power:
        Some Comments on Revolutionary
        Change." Comparative Studies in Soc.
        and Hist., 1972, 14(4): 400-421.
     b. p. 31

CHAPTER EIGHT

Q.2. a. Zahniser, Marvin R.   Uncertain
        friendship; American-French diplomatic
        relations through the cold war.
     b. Bibliographic Index, p. 176 or 490

Q.3. a. Henry Festing Jones and Augustus
        Theodore Bartholomew.   The Samuel
        Butler collection at Saint John's
        college, Cambridge.

     b. A World Bibliography of Bibliographies
        and of Bibliographical Catalogs,
        Calendars, Abstracts, Digests, Indexes
        and the Like, v. 1, c. 1071

Q.4. a. Warner, Oliver. Nelson's battles.
        Annapolis, U.S. Naval Institute, 1971.
     b. Subject Catalog; A Cumulative List of
        Works Represented by Library of
        Congress Printed Cards, v. 65, p. 39

CHAPTER NINE

Q.2. a. Franklin B. Wickwire, University of
        Massachusetts
     b. "Japanese-German Peace Negotiations
        During World War I"
     c. Paul von Hintze
     d. Leonard Gordon

Q.3. a. Annals of Wyoming
     b. Magazines for Libraries, p. 416

CHAPTER TEN

Q.2. a. American Historical Review, 80:722-3,
        June 1975, C. Eaton.
     b. p. 837

Q.3. a. Karl G. Larew
     b. Towson State University
     c. pp. 163-164

Q.4. a. Michael R. Greco
     b. San Jose State University
     c. pp. 322-327

CHAPTER ELEVEN

Q.2. a. Alert
     b. 1882
     c. p. 899

Q.3. a. Amer Jewish Com yr-end rept on plight of
        Jews in Moslem world notes biggest
        Jewish populations remain in Iran,
        Morocco, Turkey and Tunisia and that
        govts have maintained basic human
        rights and security
     b. Ja 2,5:1
     c. p. 2206

Q.4. a. Commissioner--report criticizes Somerset
        hospital over doctor's 67 hour shift
     b. July 4, 2d
     c. p. 153

CHAPTER TWELVE

Q.2. a. Division of Economic Development.
        Scenic & historic tours of New Jersey;
        crossroads of the Revolution [Prepared
        by the Office of Tourism and Promotion
        in cooperation with the New Jersey
        American Revolution Bicentennial
        Celebration Commission and the New
        Jersey Dept. of Transportation.
        Trenton, n. d.] 36 p. illus.
     b. Monthly Checklist of State Publications,
        p. 1033

Q.3. a. Connecticut. State Library, Hartford.
        Checklist of publications of
        Connecticut state agencies received by
        the Connecticut State Library. April
        1964+ Hartford. monthly
     b. Government Publications: A Guide to
        Bibliographical Tools, p. 93

Q.4. a. (63) 8859
     b. Liberation of Belgrade (Oct. 1944).
        April 2, 1963. [2]+24 p.

MATERIALS & METHODS
FOR
HISTORY RESEARCH

Answer by Book

Book No. __6__

CHAPTER ONE

Q.2. a. Sources of business information
b. Guide to Reference Books, p. 504

Q.3. a. A New Dictionary of British History
b. The Historian's Handbook: A Descriptive
Guide to Reference Works, p. 79

Q.4. a. Medieval agrarian economy
b. Guide to Historical Literature, p. 191

Q.5. a. Tragic Years, 1860-1865
b. Harvard Guide to American History,
p. 864

CHAPTER TWO

Q.2. a. $258,682,187 (in $1,000)
b. Historical Statistics of the United
States; Colonial Times to 1970,
p. 1117

Q.3. a. Oregon Settlement
b. Encyclopedia of American History, p. 232

Q.4. a. June 8, 1815
b. Encyclopedia of World History, p. 651

CHAPTER THREE

Q.2. a. Georges Salomon
4400-17th St., NW,
Washington, D.C. 20011
b. Statesman's Yearbook; Statistical and
Historical Annual of the States of
the World, p. 1013

Q.3. a. $247 million
b. Statistical Abstract of the United
States, p. 263

Q.4. a. 7 263; 2 467 (million Marks)
b. Statistical Yearbook, p. 708

Q.5. a. Bentsen quits Presidential Race
b. World Almanac, p. 920

Q.6. a. N. A. F. St. John-Stevas, Conservative
b. Whitaker's Almanack, p. 327

CHAPTER FOUR

Q.2. a. Plate 133, Tullahoma to Atlanta, 1863-
1864
b. Atlas of American History

Q.3. a. Historical Atlas of the United States
b. Map no. 103, p. 70

Q.4. a. Historical Atlas
b. p. 8, 1:36,000,000

CHAPTER FIVE

Q.2. a. Dictionary of American History, v. 3,
p. 17
b. Fort Phil Kearny

Q.3. a. F. P. Braudel and F. Spooner
b. Cambridge Economic History of Europe,
pp. 605-615

Q.4. a. A. C. Crombie & Michael Hoskin
b. Change in scientific movement
c. New Cambridge Modern History, v. 6

CHAPTER SIX

Q.2. a. Spain, 1536-?1602
b. Webster's Biographical Dictionary,
p. 515

Q.3. a. ironmaster
b. Dictionary of National Biography, v. 6,
p. 99 or v. 16, p. 99

Q.4. a. Hist. of Chicago
b. Dictionary of American Biography, v. 6,
pp. 294-5

Q.5. a. U. of Pennsylvania
b. Directory of American Scholars, p. 201

CHAPTER SEVEN

Q.3. a. News from China: seventeenth-century
European notices of the Manchu
conquest. E. J. Van Kley. Journal of
Modern History 45:561-82 D'73.
b. p. 74

Q.4. a. Utley, Robert M. "The Suicide Fight."
Am. Hist. Illus., 1971, 6(8): 41-43.
b. America: History and Life, p. 38

Q.5. a. Smith, Robert H. T., ed. "Spatial
Structure and Process in Tropical West
Africa." Econ. Geography, 1972, 48(3):
b. p. 41

CHAPTER EIGHT

Q.2. a. Nicholas, Herbert George. United States
and Britain.
b. Bibliographic Index, p. 204 or 490

Q.3. a. Jessie Parkhurst Guzman. George
Washington Carver. A classified
bibliography.
b. A World Bibliography of Bibliographies
and of Bibliographical Catalogs,
Calendars, Abstracts, Digests, Indexes
and the Like, v. 1, c. 1168

CHAPTER EIGHT, continued

Q.4. a. Thiry, Jean. Marengo. Paris, Berger-
Levrault, 1949.
b. <u>Subject Catalog; A Cumulative List of
Works Represented by Library of
Congress Printed Cards</u>, v. 57, p. 415

CHAPTER NINE

Q.2. a. Lynn White, Jr., University of
California-Los Angeles
b. "Noncapitalist Wealth and the Origins of
the French Revolution"
c. San Francisco
d. B. G. Gokhale

Q.3. a. Arizona and the West: a quarterly
journal of history
b. <u>Magazines for Libraries</u>, p. 417

CHAPTER TEN

Q.2. a. <u>Journal of American History</u>, 62:375-6,
September 1975, W. Chazanof.
b. p. 913

Q.3. a. Dennis Showalter
b. Colorado College
c. pp. 175-176

Q.4. a. Ann J. Lane
b. John Jay College, CUNY
c. pp. 438-442

CHAPTER ELEVEN

Q.2. a. Free Press
b. 1892
c. p. 897

Q.3. a. Group of Northport (NY) HS students
'adopts' B M Kamara, pol prisoner in
Sierra Leone
b. Ja 14,35:1
c. p. 1976

Q.4. a. Administrative staff--work-to-rule
called off
b. Jan. 7, 1c
c. p. 152

CHAPTER TWELVE

Q.2. a. <u>Legislature. Commission on Expenditure
Review. State historic preservation
programs.</u> [Albany] 1974. S 15, iv,
124 p. illus.
b. <u>Monthly Checklist of State Publications</u>,
p. 641

Q.3. a. Delaware. <u>Public Archives Commission.
List of accessions.</u> v. 1+ Oct. 1951+
Dover.
b. <u>Government Publications: A Guide to
Bibliographical Tools</u>, p. 94

Q.4. a. (67) 11992
b. Reports of General MacArthur: v. 2,
Japanese operations in southwest
Pacific Area. [1967] xiv+363+[1]
p. xii+365-803 p.

MATERIALS & METHODS
FOR
HISTORY RESEARCH

Answer by Book

Book No. ___7___

CHAPTER ONE

Q.2. a. <u>Searching the chemical literature</u>
b. <u>Guide to Reference Books</u>, p. 734

Q.3. a. <u>The Modern Encyclopedia of Australia and New Zealand</u>
b. <u>The Historian's Handbook: A Descriptive Guide to Reference Works</u>, p. 85

Q.4. a. <u>Business in the Middle Ages</u>
b. <u>Guide to Historical Literature</u>, p. 194

Q.5. a. <u>Politics of Reconstruction, 1863-1867</u>
b. <u>Harvard Guide to American History</u>, p. 879

CHAPTER TWO

Q.2. a. $269,422,099 (in $1,000)
b. <u>Historical Statistics of the United States; Colonial Times to 1970</u>, p. 1117

Q.3. a. Independent Treasury Act
b. <u>Encyclopedia of American History</u>, p. 233

Q.4. a. British, 1917, Jewish homeland in Palestine
b. <u>Encyclopedia of World History</u>, p. 1091

CHAPTER THREE

Q.2. a. Roberto Lazarus
4715-16th St., NW,
Washington, D.C. 20011
b. <u>Statesman's Yearbook; Statistical and Historical Annual of the States of the World</u>, p. 1017

Q.3. a. $837 million
b. <u>Statistical Abstract of the United States</u>, p. 263

Q.4. a. 112.2; 99.3 (000 million Drachmas)
b. <u>Statistical Yearbook</u>, p. 708

Q.5. a. Ford, Carter take New Hampshire Primary

Q.6. a. E. J. Fletcher, Labour
b. <u>Whitaker's Almanack</u>, p. 328

CHAPTER FOUR

Q.2. a. Plate 63, Dunmore's War, 1774
b. <u>Atlas of American History</u>

Q.3. a. <u>Historical Atlas of the United States</u>
b. Map no. 104, p. 70

Q.4. a. <u>Historical Atlas</u>
b. p. 8, 1:36,000,000

CHAPTER FIVE

Q.2. a. <u>Dictionary of American History</u>, v. 3, p. 189
b. John G. Carlisle

Q.3. a. E. B. Fryde and M. M. Fryde
b. <u>Cambridge Economic History of Europe</u>, pp. 647-671

Q.4. a. R. R. Betts
b. Poland, Hungary, Bohemia: extent and divisions of the kingdoms
c. <u>New Cambridge Modern History</u>, v. 2

CHAPTER SIX

Q.2. a. Portugal, 1469?-1524
b. <u>Webster's Biographical Dictionary</u>, p. 573

Q.3. a. composer
b. <u>Dictionary of National Biography</u>, v. 7, p. 1140 or v. 21, p. 261

Q.4. a. <u>Hist. of Baltimore City and County</u>
b. <u>Dictionary of American Biography</u>, v. 7, pp. 176-7

Q.5. a. Harvard
b. <u>Directory of American Scholars</u>, p. 215

CHAPTER SEVEN

Q.3. a. Bicentennial perspective: religion in the American revolution. D. M. Kelley. Christianity and Crisis 34:123-8, Je 10 '74.
b. p. 486

Q.4. a. Grant, H. Roger. "The Society of Bethel: A Visitor's Account." <u>Missouri Hist. R.</u>, 1974, 68(2): 223-231.
b. <u>America: History and Life</u>, p. 206

Q.4. a. Grant, H. Roger. "The Society of Bethel: A Visitor's Account." <u>Missouri Hist. R.</u>, 1974, 68(2): 223-231.
b. <u>America: History and Life</u>, p. 206

Q.5. a. Firestone, Ya'akov. "The Doctrine of Integration with France among the Europeans of Algeria, 1955-1960." <u>Comparative Pol. Studies</u>, 1971, 4(2): 177-203.
b. p. 286

CHAPTER EIGHT

Q.2. a. Ali, Sheikh Rustum. Saudi Arabia and
          oil diplomacy.
      b. Bibliographic Index, p. 421 or 490

Q.3. a. Ludwig Lauerhass. Communism in Latin
          America. A bibliography...(1945-1960).
      b. A World Bibliography of Bibliographies
          and of Bibliographical Catalogs,
          Calendars, Abstracts, Digests, Indexes
          and the Like, v. 1, c. 1439

Q.4. a. Tetlow, Edwin. The enigma of Hasting.
          New York, St. Martin's Press, 1974.
      b. Subject Catalog; A Cumulative List of
          Works Represented by Library of
          Congress Printed Cards, v. 40, p. 405

CHAPTER NINE

Q.2. a. Lamar Cecil, University of North
          Carolina, Chapel Hill
      b. "For God, for China and for Yale--The
          Open Door in Action"
      c. 1967
      d. Ronald Inden

Q.3. a. Arkansas Historical Quarterly
      b. Magazines for Libraries, p. 417

CHAPTER TEN

Q.2. a. Journal of American History, 62:425-7,
          September 1975, P. Kleppner.
      b. p. 968

Q.3. a. Ronald J. Jensen
      b. George Mason University
      c. p. 133

Q.4. a. Robert A. Divine
      b. University of Texas
      c. pp. 507-510

CHAPTER ELEVEN

Q.2. a. Democrat-Tribune
      b. 1864
      c. p. 909

Q.3. a. Dahomey's '71 econ rev (Econ Survey of
          Africa); tourist potential of country,
          as possible factor in '72 econ
          forecast, discussed
      b. Ja 31, 51:1
      c. p. 529

Q.4. a. Administration--Green Paper published
      b. Feb. 12, 2h, 4c
      c. p. 103

CHAPTER TWELVE

Q.2. a. Division of Archives and History.
          Report. 35th; 1972/74 Raleigh. 195 p.
          illus. biennial. OR Division of
          Archives and History Archaeology
          Section. North Carolina Archaeological
          Council publication. Raleigh.
      b. Monthly Checklist of State Publications,
          p. 386

Q.3. a. Florida public documents. Feb. 1968+
          Tallahassee, Florida State Library.
          Issued monthly, with annual
          cumulations.
      b. Government Publications: A Guide to
          Bibliographical Tools, p. 96

Q.4. a. (69) 12991
      b. Liberation of Guam. [1969.] [24] p.

MATERIALS & METHODS
FOR
HISTORY RESEARCH

Answer by Book

Book No. 8

CHAPTER ONE

Q.2. a. The literature of geography; a guide to
        its organization and use
     b. Guide to Reference Books, p. 573

Q.3. a. Biographical Dictionaries and Related
        Works
     b. The Historian's Handbook: A Descriptive
        Guide to Reference Works, pp. 146-147

Q.4. a. The early history of deposit banking in
        Mediterranean Europe
     b. Guide to Historical Literature, p. 195

Q.5. a. Water for the Cities: History of the
        Urban Water Supply Problem in the
        United States
     b. Harvard Guide to American History,
        p. 899

CHAPTER TWO

Q.2. a. $258,286,383 (in $1,000)
     b. Historical Statistics of the United
        States; Colonial Times to 1970,
        p. 1117

Q.3. a. Bryan's "Cooling Off" Treaties
     b. Encyclopedia of American History, p. 356

Q.4. a. Extended Roman citizenship to all free
        inhabitants of the empire
     b. Encyclopedia of World History, p. 128

CHAPTER THREE

Q.2. a. Ardeshir Zahedi
        3005 Massachusetts Ave., NW,
        Washington, D.C. 20008
     b. Statesman's Yearbook; Statistical and
        Historical Annual of the States of the
        World, p. 1046

Q.3. a. $881 million
     b. Statistical Abstract of the United
        States, p. 263

Q.4. a. 383; 153 (000 million Francs)
     b. Statistical Yearbook, p. 708

Q.5. a. Massachusetts primary--Jackson wins,
        Carter 4th
     b. World Almanac, p. 923

Q.6. a. M. H. Thatcher, Conservative
     b. Whitaker's Almanack, p. 331

CHAPTER FOUR

Q.2. a. Plate 125, Civil War, 1861-1865
     b. Atlas of American History

Q.3. a. Historical Atlas of the United States
     b. Map no. 220, p. 145

Q.4. a. Historical Atlas
     b. p. 9, 1:4,000,000

CHAPTER FIVE

Q.2. a. Dictionary of American History, v. 2,
        p. 241
     b. Confederate States

Q.3. a. Courtenay Edward Stevens
     b. Cambridge Economic History of Europe,
        pp. 755-761

Q.4. a. E. G. Rupp
     b. Luther: his birth, early life and
        education
     c. New Cambridge Modern History, v. 2

CHAPTER SIX

Q.2. a. Germany, 1863-1919
     b. Webster's Biographical Dictionary,
        p. 647

Q.3. a. professor of physic
     b. Dictionary of National Biography, v. 8,
        p. 24 or v. 22, p. 24

Q.4. a. Life and Pub. Services of Thos. A.
        Hendricks
     b. Dictionary of American Biography, v. 8,
        pp. 534-5

Q.5. a. Johns Hopkins U.
     b. Directory of American Scholars, p. 289

CHAPTER SEVEN

Q.3. a. Local initiative and finance in
        defense of the viceroyalty of Peru:
        the development of self-reliance.
        L. A. Clayton. Hispanic American
        Historical Review 54:284-304 My '74.
     b. p. 318

Q.4. a. Kelsey, Harry. "The Doolittle Report of
        1867: Its Preparation and
        Shortcomings." Arizona and the West,
        1975, 17(2): 107-120.
     b. America: History and Life, p. 308

CHAPTER SEVEN, continued

Q.5. a. Pankhurst, Richard. "The Ethiopian
          National Anthem in 1940: A Chapter in
          Anglo-Ethiopian Wartime Relations."
          Ethiopian Observer [Egypt], 1971,
          14(3): 219-225.
       b. p. 264

CHAPTER EIGHT

Q.2. a. Warnock, John W. Partner to behemoth;
          the military policy of a satelite
          Canada.
       b. Bibliographic Index, p. 64 or 466

Q.3. a. James Truslow Adams. Bibliography of
          the writings of Henry Adams.
       b. A World Bibliography of Bibliographies
          and of Bibliographical Catalogs,
          Calendars, Abstracts, Digests, Indexes
          and the Like, v. 1, c. 125

Q.4. a. Featherstone, Donald F. Poitiers, 1356.
          London, C. Knight, 1972.
       b. Subject Catalog; A Cumulative List of
          Works Represented by Library of
          Congress Printed Cards, v. 71, p. 158

CHAPTER NINE

Q.2. a. Marc Raeff, Columbia University
       b. "Underlying Themes in the Witchcraft of
          Seventeenth-Century New England"
       c. April, 1967
       d. Sylvia L. Thrupp

Q.3. a. California Historical Quarterly, the
          journal of the California Historical
          Society
       b. Magazines for Libraries, p. 417

CHAPTER TEN

Q.2. a. Historical Journal, 18:417-20, June
          1975, H. Brogan.
       b. p. 838

Q.3. a. John A. Carpenter
       b. Fordham University
       c. p. 107

Q.4. a. Joseph Frazier Wall
       b. Grinnell College
       c. pp. 339-343

CHAPTER ELEVEN

Q.2. a. Tribune-Keystone
       b. 1886
       c. p. 901

Q.3. a. Mali's '71 econ rev (Econ Survey of
          Africa); Govt's efforts to realign
          econ since Pres Traore's mil regime
          overthrew former Govt in '68 discussed
       b. Ja 31,52:1
       c. p. 1205

Q.4. a. Administration--legislation expected
       b. Oct. 29, 4d
       c. p. 101

CHAPTER TWELVE

Q.2. a. Coastal Conservation and Development
          Commission. Historical and
          archaeological resources of the Oregon
          coastal zone; a resource inventory
          report, prepared by Stephen Dow
          Beckham, assisted by Donna Lee Hepp.
          [Florence] 1974. 41 p. illus.
       b. Monthly Checklist of State Publications,
          p. 864

Q.3. a. Georgia. State Library, Atlanta.
          Checklist of official publications of
          the state of Georgia. Feb./Aug. 1954+
          Atlanta. quarterly.
       b. Government Publications: A Guide to
          Bibliographical Tools, p. 98

Q.4. a. (65) 11381
       b. United States Army in World War II:
          European theater of operations [v. 8],
          Ardennes, Battle of the Bulge. 1965.
          xxii+[1]+720 p.

MATERIALS & METHODS
FOR
HISTORY RESEARCH

Answer by Book

Book No. 9

CHAPTER ONE

Q.2. a. Sources of information for the
literature of geology; an introductory
guide
b. Guide to Reference Books, p. 744

Q.3. a. Columbia Lippincott Gazetteer of the
World
b. The Historian's Handbook: A Descriptive
Guide to Reference Works, pp. 130-131

Q.4. a. History of Christian philosophy in the
Middle Ages
b. Guide to Historical Literature, p. 198

Q.5. a. Business Cycle Theory in the United
States, 1860-1900
b. Harvard Guide to American History, p. 901

CHAPTER TWO

Q.2. a. $252,292,247 (in $1,000)
b. Historical Statistics of the United
States; Colonial Times to 1970,
p. 1117

Q.3. a. Mann-Elkins Act
b. Encyclopedia of American History, p. 322

Q.4. a. 1905-1907
b. Encyclopedia of World History, p. 761

CHAPTER THREE

Q.2. a. Khalid M. Jaffar
2940 Tilden St., NW,
Washington, D.C. 20008

b. Statesman's Yearbook; Statistical and
Historical Annual of the States of
the World, p. 1115

Q.3. a. $139 million
b. Statistical Abstract of the United
States, p. 263

Q.4. a. 59 150; 18 801 (000 million Lire)
b. Statistical Yearbook, p. 709

Q.5. a. Ford wins Florida primary; Carter beats
Wallace
b. World Almanac, p. 923

Q.6. a. D. R. Johnston, Liberal
b. Whitaker's Almanack, p. 334

CHAPTER FOUR

Q.2. a. Plate 132, Chickamauga and Chattanooga,
1863
b. Atlas of American History

Q.3. a. Historical Atlas of the United States
b. Map no. 221, p. 145

Q.4. a. Historical Atlas
b. p. 12, 1:20,000,000

CHAPTER FIVE

Q.2. a. Dictionary of American History, v. 2,
p. 379
b. The Fighting Cheyennes

Q.3. a. H. van Werveke
b. Cambridge Economic History of Europe,
pp. 605-608

Q.4. a. J. M. Batista i Roca
b. Castile: population and economy
c. New Cambridge Modern History, v. 1

CHAPTER SIX

Q.2. a. Chile, 1877-1960
b. Webster's Biographical Dictionary,
p. 753

Q.3. a. statesman
b. Dictionary of National Biography, v. 9,
p. 1056 or v. 27, p. 162

Q.4. a. The Wanderer Case
b. Dictionary of American Biography, v. 9,
p. 543

Q.5. a. Princeton
b. Directory of American Scholars, p. 309

CHAPTER SEVEN

Q.3. a. Jorge Ubico and the Belice boundary
dispute. K. J. Grieb. Americas
30:448-74 Ap '74.
b. p. 39

Q.4. a. Miller, M. Sammy. "The Negro in
Delaware." Negro Hist. Bull., 1973,
36(3): 66-67.
b. America: History and Life, p. 411

Q.5. a. Mehmet, Ozay. "Effectiveness of Foreign
Aid--The Case of Somalia." J. of
Modern African Studies [South Africa],
1971, 9(1): 31-47.
b. p. 37

CHAPTER EIGHT

Q.2. a. Bonsal, Philip Wilson. Cuba, Castro, and the United States.
   b. <u>Bibliographic Index</u>, p. 109 or 466

Q.3. a. Henry Martyn Dexter. The Congregationalism of the last three hundred years as seen in its literature.
   b. <u>A World Bibliography of Bibliographies and of Bibliographical Catalogs, Calendars, Abstracts, Digests, Indexes and the Like</u>, v. 1, c. 1469

Q.4. a. Brett-James, Antony. comp. Europe against Napoleon: the Leipzig Campaign, 1813, from eyewitness accounts. London, Macmillan, 1970.
   b. <u>Subject Catalog; A Cumulative List of Works Represented by Library of Congress Printed Cards</u>, v. 54, p. 131

CHAPTER NINE

Q.2. a. Maury Klein, University of Rhode Island
   b. "The Unification of Germany in East German Perspective"
   c. 1866-1871
   d. Raymond G. O'Connor

Q.3. a. Kansas Historical Quarterly
   b. <u>Magazines for Libraries</u>, p. 418

CHAPTER TEN

Q.2. a. <u>Hispanic American Historical Review</u>, 55:602-3, August 1975, J. J. Tepaske.
   b. p. 967

Q.3. a. H. S. Reinmuth, Jr.
   b. University of Akron
   c. pp. 94-95

Q.4. a. Eric Foner
   b. City College, CUNY
   c. pp. 77-81

CHAPTER ELEVEN

Q.2. a. Courier-Wedge
   b. 1861
   c. p. 900

Q.3. a. Pres Mobutu renames several well-known places in Zaire; Kinshasa Prov to be known as Shaba; Stanley Pool renamed Malebo Pool; Mt Stanley renamed Mt Ngaliema
   b. Ja 2,8:1
   c. p. 2560

Q.4. a. Administration--doctors dissatisfied with Green Paper
   b. Jan. 23, 2g
   c. p. 95

CHAPTER TWELVE

Q.2. a. <u>Dept. of Archives and History</u>. South Carolina historic preservation plan. Vol. 3. Preservation program. 1975/76. Columbia. 75 p. illus. annual.
   b. <u>Monthly Checklist of State Publications</u>, p. 962

Q.3. a. Hawaii documents. no. 1/2+ Jan./Feb. 1967+ [Honolulu] Hawaii State Library. bi-monthly, annual cumulation. OR Current Hawaiiana. v. 1+ June 1944+ [Honolulu] quarterly.
   b. <u>Government Publications: A Guide to Bibliographical Tools</u>, p. 98

Q.4. a. (51) 3865
   b. Assault on Peleliu. [1950.] v+209 p.

MATERIALS & METHODS
FOR
HISTORY RESEARCH

Answer by Book

Book No. __10__

CHAPTER ONE

Q.2. a. The law in the United States of
America; a selective bibliographical
guide
b. Guide to Reference Books, p. 553

Q.3. a. Political Africa
b. The Historian's Handbook: A Descriptive
Guide to Reference Works, p. 167

Q.4. a. The growth of political thought in the
West: from the Greeks to the end of
the Middle Ages
b. Guide to Historical Literature, p. 199

Q.5. a. Principles of Foreign Policy under the
Cleveland Administrations
b. Harvard Guide to American History,
p. 913

CHAPTER TWO

Q.2. a. $252,770,360 (in $1,000)
b. Historical Statistics of the United
States; Colonial Times to 1970,
p. 1117

Q.3. a. Canadian Reciprocity Treaty
b. Encyclopedia of American History, p. 258

Q.4. a. De nova Hierosolyma
b. Encyclopedia of World History,
pp. 521-522

CHAPTER THREE

Q.2. a. Abdelhadi Boutaleb
1601 21st St., NW,
Washington, D.C. 20009
b. Statesman's Yearbook; Statistical and
Historical Annual of the States of the
World, p. 1162

Q.3. a. $1,501 million
b. Statistical Abstract of the United
States, p. 263

Q.4. a. 4 036; 1 789 (million Shillings)
b. Statistical Yearbook, p. 709

Q.5. a. Ford wins Illinois primary; Carter wins
48% of vote
b. World Almanac, p. 923

Q.6. a. J. J. Wells, Conservative
b. Whitaker's Almanack, p. 336

CHAPTER FOUR

Q.2. a. Plate 74, The Revolutionary War in the
South
b. Atlas of American History

Q.3. a. Historical Atlas of the United States
b. Map no. 222, p. 146

Q.4. a. Historical Atlas
b. p. 16, 1:500,000

CHAPTER FIVE

Q.2. a. Dictionary of American History, v. 1,
pp. 342-343
b. Long Walk

Q.3. a. R. de Roover
b. Cambridge Economic History of Europe,
pp. 608-612

Q.4. a. R. Weiss
b. Humanism in Italy: local characteristics
c. New Cambridge Modern History, v. 1

CHAPTER SIX

Q.2. a. Germany, 1854-1938
b. Webster's Biographical Dictionary,
p. 808

Q.3. a. architect
b. Dictionary of National Biography, v. 10,
p. 999 or v. 30, p. 111

Q.4. a. Thomas Joy and His Descendants
b. Dictionary of American Biography, v. 10,
pp. 224-5

Q.5. a. New York U.
b. Directory of American Scholars, p. 339

CHAPTER SEVEN

Q.3. a. Social welfare and the Edict of
Nantes: Lyon and Nimes. W. J. Pugh.
French Historical Studies 8:349-76
Spr '74.
b. p. 126

Q.4. a. Keuchel, Edward F. "A Purely Business
Motive: German-American Lumber Company,
1901-1918." Florida Hist. Q., 1974,
52(4): 381-395.
b. America: History and Life, p. 412

CHAPTER SEVEN, continued

Q.5. a. Robertson, A. F. "Party Politics and a
        Rural Immigrant Community." *Journal
        of Modern African Studies* [South
        Africa], 1971, 9(1): 124-130.
     b. p. 38

CHAPTER EIGHT

Q.2. a. Davis, Lynn Etheridge. Cold war
        begins; Soviet-Am. conflict over
        Eastern Europe.
     b. *Bibliographic Index*, p. 154 or 466

Q.3. a. Aziz Suryal Atiya. The Crusade,
        historiography and bibliography.
     b. *A World Bibliography of Bibliographies
        and of Bibliographical Catalogs,
        Calendars, Abstracts, Digests, Indexes
        and the Like*, v. 1, c. 1535

Q.4. a. Lloyd, Alan. Marathon: the story of
        civilizations on collision course.
        1st ed. New York, Random House, 1973.
     b. *Subject Catalog; A Cumulative List of
        Works Represented by Library of
        Congress Printed Cards*, v. 57, p. 403

CHAPTER NINE

Q.2. a. Roger A. Fischer, Sam Houston State
        College
     b. "Southern Violence"
     c. 73.2
     d. F. E. Peters

Q.3. a. Maryland Historian
     b. *Magazines for Libraries*, p. 418

CHAPTER TEN

Q.2. a. *Journal of Southern History*, 41:91-2,
        February 1975, D. J. Berthrong.
     b. p. 910

Q.3. a. Dennis Reinhartz
     b. University of Texas at Arlington
     c. p. 215

Q.4. a. Peter Kolchin
     b. University of Wisconsin-Madison
     c. pp. 228-236

CHAPTER ELEVEN

Q.2. a. Blade-Atlas
     b. 1888
     c. p. 898

Q.3. a. S W Kapwepwe, former Vice Pres of
        Zambia, who heads United Progressive
        Party in opposition to Pres Kaunda, is
        beaten by crowd, Lusaka; most other
        leaders of Progressive Party were
        arrested 3 mos ago but have not been
        brought to trial
     b. Ja 13,16:3
     c. p. 2560

Q.4. a. Administration--revised Green Paper to
        be issued
     b. Mar. 1, 3c
     c. p. 90

CHAPTER TWELVE

Q.2. a. *Historical Commission*. Report.
        1973-74. [Austin] unpaged.
        illus. biennial.
     b. *Monthly Checklist of State Publications*,
        p. 879

Q.3. a. Illinois. *Secretary of State*.
        Publications of the state of Illinois.
        [Springfield]. Illinois documents
        list. Mar. 15, 1971+ Springfield,
        Illinois State Library, Documents
        Unit. semimonthly.
     b. *Government Publications: A Guide to
        Bibliographical Tools*, p. 100

Q.4. a. (60) 2076
     b. United States Army in World War II:
        China-Burma-India theater [v. 3], Time
        runs out in CBI. 1959. xvii+428 p.

MATERIALS & METHODS
FOR
HISTORY RESEARCH

Answer by Book

Book No. ___11___

CHAPTER ONE

Q.2. a. A guide to information sources in
mining, minerals, and geosciences
b. Guide to Reference Books, p. 753

Q.3. a. Australian Dictionary of Biography
b. The Historian's Handbook: A Descriptive
Guide to Reference Works p. 163

Q.4. a. A history of medieval Latin literature
b. Guide to Historical Literature, p. 200

Q.5. a. American Catholicism and Social Action,
1865-1950
b. Harvard Guide to American History,
p. 931

CHAPTER TWO

Q.2. a. $257,357,352 (in $1,000)
b. Historical Statistics of the United
States; Colonial Times to 1970,
p. 1117

Q.3. a. Hay-Pauncefote Treaty
b. Encyclopedia of American History, p. 348

Q.4. a. Pius IX (indexed as Papacy...
infallibility)
b. Encyclopedia of World History, p. 713

CHAPTER THREE

Q.2. a. Guillermo Sevilla-Sacasa
1627 New Hampshire Avenue, NW,
Washington, D.C. 20009
b. Statesman's Yearbook; Statistical and
Historical Annual of the States of the
World, p. 1188

Q.3. a. $5,682 million
b. Statistical Abstract of the United
States, p. 263

Q.4. a. 77.3; 59.0 (million Kwacha)
b. Statistical Yearbook, p. 709

Q.5. a. North Carolina primary--Reagan
defeated Ford; Carter beat Wallace
b. World Almanac, p. 923

Q.6. a. E. S. Bishop, Labour
b. Whitaker's Almanack, p. 337

CHAPTER FOUR

Q.2. a. Plate 96, War of 1812, Lake Region
b. Atlas of American History

Q.3. a. Historical Atlas of the United States
b. Map no. 39, p. 29

Q.4. a. Historical Atlas
b. pp. 18-19, 1:18,000,000

CHAPTER FIVE

Q.2. a. Dictionary of American History, v. 1,
p. 213
b. State of Rhode Island and Providence
Plantations

Q.3. a. A. B. Hibbert
b. Cambridge Economic History of Europe,
pp. 614-624

Q.4. a. Gordon Craig
b. The diplomatic division of Europe
c. New Cambridge Modern History, v. 10

CHAPTER SIX

Q.2. a. Canada, 1807-1864
b. Webster's Biographical Dictionary,
p. 848

Q.3. a. painter
b. Dictionary of National Biography, v. 11,
p. 240 or v. 31, p. 240

Q.4. a. Minutes of the Council and Gen. Court of
Colonial Va.
b. Dictionary of American Biography, v. 11,
pp. 496-7

Q.5. a. U. of California
b. Directory of American Scholars, p. 361

CHAPTER SEVEN

Q.2. a. Daladier and the Munich crisis: a
reappraisal. S. B. Butterworth.
Journal of Contemporary History
9:191-216 Jl '74.
b. p. 308

Q.4. a. Pearce, George F. "Assessing Public
Opinion: Editorial Comment and the
Annexation of Hawaii--A Case Study."
Pacific Hist. R., 1974, 43(3):
324-341.
b. America: History and Life, p. 217

CHAPTER SEVEN, continued

Q.5. a. Trout, Frank E. "Morocco's Boundary in
the Guir-Zousfana River Basin."
<u>African Hist. Studies</u>, 1970, 3(1):
37-56.
b. p. 36

CHAPTER EIGHT

Q.2. a. Kennedy, Paul Michael. Samoan tangle;
a study in Anglo-German-Am. relations,
1878-1900.
b. <u>Bibliographic Index</u>, p. 191 or 466

Q.3. a. Enok Mortensen. Danish-American life
and letters. A bibliography.
b. <u>A World Bibliography of Bibliographies
and of Bibliographical Catalogs,
Calendars, Abstracts, Digests, Indexes
and the Like</u>, v. 4, c. 6324

Q.4. a. Herold, J. Christopher. The Battle of
Waterloo, by the editors of Horizon
Magazine. London, Cassell, 1967.
b. <u>Subject Catalog; A Cumulative List of
Works Represented by Library of
Congress Printed Cards</u>, v. 41, p. 662

CHAPTER NINE

Q.2. a. Edmund S. Morgan, Yale University
b. "The Cold War and the Election of 1948"
c. American Philosophical Society
d. John Haskell Kemble

Q.3. a. Montana, the Magazine of Western History
b. <u>Magazines for Libraries</u>, p. 419

CHAPTER TEN

Q.2. a. <u>Journal of American History</u>, 62:441-2,
September 1975, R. A. Esthus.
b. p. 945

Q.3. a. Gerald Cavanaugh
b. George Mason University
c. pp. 87-88

Q.4. a. Howard P. Chudacoff
b. Brown University
c. pp. 99-104

CHAPTER ELEVEN

Q.2. a. Reporter
b. 1884
c. p. 903

Q.3. a. '70 econ rev, '71 outlook; illus
b. Ja 29,54:4
c. p. 656

Q.4. a. Executive Council Assn. conf.
b. Oct. 21, 2h
c. p. 95

CHAPTER TWELVE

Q.2. a. <u>State Parks and Recreation Commission.</u>
National register properties in
Washington State. [Olympia, 1974? 10]p.
illus.
b. <u>Monthly Checklist of State Publications</u>,
p. 414

Q.3. a. Indiana documents received at the State
Library. Library occurrent. Indiana
State Library, Indianapolis.
b. <u>Government Publications: A Guide to
Bibliographical Tools</u>, p. 101

Q.4. a. (66) 9356
b. Brazilian Expeditionary Force by its
Commander; [1966.] xxi+279 p.

MATERIALS & METHODS
FOR
HISTORY RESEARCH

Answer by Book

Book No. 12

CHAPTER ONE

Q.2. a. <u>Musicalia; sources of information in music</u>
     b. <u>Guide to Reference Books</u>, p. 413

Q.3. a. <u>Biographical Directory of the American Congress 1774-1961</u>
     b. <u>The Historian's Handbook: A Descriptive Guide to Reference Works</u>, pp. 170-171

Q.4. a. <u>Mediaeval Art</u>
     b. <u>Guide to Historical Literature</u>, p. 201

Q.5. a. <u>Lords of Creation</u>
     b. <u>Harvard Guide to American History</u>, p. 937

CHAPTER TWO

Q.2. a. $255,221,977 (in $1,000)
     b. <u>Historical Statistics of the United States; Colonial Times to 1970</u>, p. 1117

Q.3. a. General Amnesty Act
     b. <u>Encyclopedia of American History</u>, p. 299

Q.4. a. Karl Liebknecht, Rosa Luxemburg
     b. <u>Encyclopedia of World History</u>, p. 1005

CHAPTER THREE

Q.2. a. Sahabzada Yaqub-Khan
        2315 Massachusetts Ave., NW,
        Washington, D.C. 20008
     b. <u>Statesman's Yearbook; Statistical and Historical Annual of the States of the World</u>, p. 1213

Q.3. a. $171 million
     b. <u>Statistical Abstract of the United States</u>, p. 263

Q.4. a. 10 884; 4 621 (million Dirhams)
     b. <u>Statistical Yearbook</u>, p. 709

Q.5. a. Bayh "suspends" his campaign
     b. <u>World Almanac</u>, p. 923

Q.6. a. A. Roberts, Labour
     b. <u>Whitaker's Almanack</u>, p. 338

CHAPTER FOUR

Q.2. a. Plate 121, The Kansas-Missouri Border, 1854-1859
     b. <u>Atlas of American History</u>

Q.3. a. <u>Historical Atlas of the United States</u>
     b. Map no. 40, p. 29

Q.4. a. <u>Historical Atlas</u>
     b. p. 32, 1:20,000,000

CHAPTER FIVE

Q.2. a. <u>Dictionary of American History</u>, v. 1, p. 385
     b. <u>The Red Man in the United States</u>

Q.3. a. Sylvia L. Thrupp
     b. <u>Cambridge Economic History of Europe</u>, pp. 624-634

Q.4. a. J. A. Hawgood
     b. Changes in forms of government
     c. <u>New Cambridge Modern History</u>, v. 10

CHAPTER SIX

Q.2. a. France, 1875-1949
     b. <u>Webster's Biographical Dictionary</u>, p. 960

Q.3. a. explorer
     b. <u>Dictionary of National Biography</u>, v. 12, p. 333 or v. 34, p. 333

Q.4. a. <u>The Life and Times of C. G. Memminger</u>
     b. <u>Dictionary of American Biography</u>, v. 12, pp. 527-8

Q.5. a. U. of London
     b. <u>Directory of American Scholars</u>, p. 412

CHAPTER SEVEN

Q.3. a. Recent literature on Queen Victoria's little wars. B. D. Gooch. Victorian Studies 17:217-224 D '73.
     b. p. 102

Q.4. a. Nelson, William E. "The Legal Restraint of Power in Pre-revolutionary America: Massachusetts as a Case Study, 1760-1775." <u>Am. J. of Legal Hist.</u>, 1974, 18(1): 1-32.
     b. <u>America: History and Life</u>, p. 315

Q.5. a. Hay, Alan M. "Imports Versus Local Production: A Case Study from the Nigerian Cement Industry." <u>Econ. Geography</u>, 1971, 47(3): 384-388.
     b. pp. 39-40

CHAPTER EIGHT

Q.2. a. Jauhri, R. C. American diplomacy and
          independence for India.
      b. Bibliographic Index, p. 199 or 466

Q.3. a. Emory Stephens Bogardus. The mexican
          immigrant. An annotated bibliography.
      b. A World Bibliography of Bibliographies
          and of Bibliographical Catalogs,
          Calendars, Abstracts, Digests, Indexes
          and the Like, v. 4, c. 6325

Q.4. a. Howarth, David Armine. Trafalgar; the
          Nelson touch. 1st American ed., New
          York, Atheneum, 1969.
      b. Subject Catalog; A Cumulative List of
          Works Represented by Library of
          Congress Printed Cards, v. 39,
          p. 380

CHAPTER NINE

Q.2. a. Lois W. Banner, Rutgers University
      b. "Was There a Compromise of 1877?"
      c. 1963
      d. William Greenleaf

Q.3. a. North Dakota History; a journal of the
          Northern plains
      b. Magazines for Libraries, p. 419

CHAPTER TEN

Q.2. a. Journal of American History,
          61:1116-17, March 1975,
          R. E. Berlinger.
      b. p. 892

Q.3. a. Jerry Israel
      b. Illinois Wesleyan University
      c. p. 171

Q.4. a. Robert M. Calhoon
      b. University of North Carolina at
          Greensboro
      c. pp. 520-525

CHAPTER ELEVEN

Q.2. a. Barron Co. News-Shield
      b. 1876
      c. p. 898

Q.3. a. Govt, in further swing to left, issues
          order nationalizing all private bldgs
          worth over $14,300; move linked to
          Pres Nyerere anxiety over Uganda coup;
          map
      b. My 16,14:1
      c. p. 1595

Q.4. a. Bill--report stage
      b. Apr. 2, 5h
      c. p. 99

CHAPTER TWELVE

Q.2. a. Antiquities Commission. Report.
          10th; 1974. Morgantown. ix, 67 p.
          illus. annual.
      b. Monthly Checklist of State Publications,
          p. 678

Q.3. a. Iowa documents; list. no. 1+ Jan./Mar.
          1956+ [Iowa City] State University
          of Iowa Libraries. quarterly.
      b. Government Publications: A Guide to
          Bibliographical Tools, p. 102

Q.4. a. (57) 404
      b. Soviet partisan movement, 1941-44. Aug.
          1956. x+217 p.

MATERIALS & METHODS
FOR
HISTORY RESEARCH

Answer by Book

Book No. __13__

CHAPTER ONE

Q.2. a. How to find out in philosophy and
         psychology
     b. Guide to Reference Books, p. 245

Q.3. a. The Justices of the Supreme Court, 1789-
         1969: Their Lives and Major Opinions
     b. The Historian's Handbook: A Descriptive
         Guide to Reference Works, p. 172

Q.4. a. Roman Britain and the Roman army
     b. Guide to Historical Literature, p. 155

Q.5. a. Churchill, Roosevelt, Stalin: The War
         They Waged and the Peace They Sought
     b. Harvard Guide to American History,
         p. 1008

CHAPTER TWO

Q.2. a. $259,105,179 (in $1,000)
     b. Historical Statistics of the United
         States; Colonial Times to 1970,
         p. 1117

Q.3. a. Electoral Count Act
     b. Encyclopedia of American History, p. 308

Q.4. a. the Prussians
     b. Encyclopedia of World History, p. 503

CHAPTER THREE

Q.2. a. Abdullah Saleh Al-Mana
         60 New Hampshire Avenue, NW,
         Washington, D.C. 20037
     b. Statesman's Yearbook; Statistical and
         Historical Annual of the States of the
         World, p. 1262

Q.3. a. $714 million
     b. Statistical Abstract of the United
         States, p. 263

Q.4. a. 39.4; 13.6 (000 million Guilders)
     b. Statistical Yearbook, p. 710

Q.5. a. Shapp withdraws
     b. World Almanac, p. 923

Q.6. a. L. Abse, Labour
     b. Whitaker's Almanack, p. 339

CHAPTER FOUR

Q.2. a. Plate 134, Memphis to the Gulf, 1862-
         1863
     b. Atlas of American History

Q.3. a. Historical Atlas of the United States
     b. Map no. 106, p. 71

Q.4. a. Historical Atlas
     b. p. 20, 1:8,000,000

CHAPTER FIVE

Q.2. a. Dictionary of American History, v. 6,
         pp. 195-6
     b. Three Years Among the Indians and
         Mexicans

Q.3. a. E. E. Rich
     b. Cambridge Economic History of Europe,
         pp. 602-605

Q.4. a. George Clark
     b. Europe's 'military revolution'
     c. New Cambridge Modern History, v. 5

CHAPTER SIX

Q.2. a. Sweden, 1718-1763
     b. Webster's Biographical Dictionary,
         p. 1105

Q.3. a. economic writer
     b. Dictionary of National Biography, v. 13,
         p. 1183 or v. 39, p. 286

Q.4. a. Public Papers of Benjamin B. Odell
     b. Dictionary of American Biography, v. 13,
         pp. 622-3

Q.5. a. U. of Texas
     b. Directory of American Scholars, p. 467

CHAPTER SEVEN

Q.3. a. Britain, Portugal, and the first World
         war, 1914-16. J. Vincent-Smith.
         European Studies Review 4:207-38
         Jl '74.
     b. p. 144

Q.4. a. Bicha, Karel D. "The Czechs in
         Wisconsin History." Wisconsin Mag. of
         Hist., 1970, 53(3): 194-203.
     b. America: History and Life, p. 155

CHAPTER SEVEN, continued

Q.5. a. Kimmerling, Baruch. "Subsistence Crops, Cash Crops, and Urbanization: Some Materials from Ghana, Uganda, and the Ivory Coast." Rural Sociol., 1971, 36(4): 471-487.
   b. p. 258

CHAPTER EIGHT

Q.2. a. Jauhri, R. C. American diplomacy and independence for India.
   b. Bibliographic Index, p. 222 or 466

Q.3. a. Howard Drake. A bibliography of african education south of the Sahara.
   b. A World Bibliography of Bibliographies and of Bibliographical Catalogs, Calendars, Abstracts, Digests, Indexes and the Like, v. 2, c. 1848

Q.4. a. Gardiner, Samuel Rawson. The Thirty Years' War, 1618-1648. New York, Haskell House, 1968.
   b. Subject Catalog; A Cumulative List of Works Represented by Library of Congress Printed Cards, v. 39, p. 175

CHAPTER NINE

Q.2. a. Paul S. Holbo, University of Oregon
   b. "The Mythmakers of American History"
   c. Organization of American Historians
   d. Donald C. Cutter

Q.3. a. Ohio History
   b. Magazines for Libraries, p. 419

CHAPTER TEN

Q.2. a. Journal of American History, 61:1145-6, March 1975, R. E. Burton.
   b. p. 968

Q.3. a. A. J. R. Russell-Wood
   b. Johns Hopkins University
   c. pp. 127-128

Q.4. a. William Stinchcombe
   b. Syracuse University
   c. pp. 351-355

CHAPTER ELEVEN

Q.2. a. Tribune
   b. 1889
   c. p. 902

Q.3. a. Pres Bourguiba enters Walter Reed Hosp, Washington; failing health noted; illus of seaside mausoleum built for Bourguiba at his instructions
   b. Ja 7,7:4
   c. p. 1705

Q.4. a. Administrative structure--General Practitioners' Assn. views
   b. Oct. 28, 2b
   c. p. 101

CHAPTER TWELVE

Q.2. a. Division of Parks. Outdoor recreation and historic preservation in Alaska. 1973. [Anchorage] 2v. illus. annual.
   b. Monthly Checklist of State Publications, p. 471

Q.3. a. Kansas. State Library, Topeka. State Documents Division. Checklist of official publications of the state of Kansas. v. 1, no. 1+ May/Oct. 1953+ Topeka, Kans.
   b. Government Publications: A Guide to Bibliographical Tools, p. 103

Q.4. a. (63) 12819
   b. United States Army in World War II: European theater of operations [v. 7], Siegfried Line campaign. 1963. xxii+670 p.

MATERIALS & METHODS
FOR
HISTORY RESEARCH

Answer by Book

Book No. ___14___

CHAPTER ONE

Q.2. a. The literature of political science; a
       guide for students, librarians, and
       teachers
    b. Guide to Reference Books, p. 531

Q.3. a. Dod's Parliamentary Companion
    b. The Historian's Handbook: A Descriptive
       Guide to Reference Works, p. 172

Q.4. a. History and description of Roman political
       institutions
    b. Guide to Historical Literature, p. 156

Q.5. a. The Second World War
    b. Harvard Guide to American History,
       p. 1011

CHAPTER TWO

Q.2. a. $266,071,062 (in $1,000)
    b. Historical Statistics of the United
       States; Colonial Times to 1970,
       p. 1117

Q.3. a. Hatch Act
    b. Encyclopedia of American History, p. 310

Q.4. a. Japanese succession to German rights in
       Shantung
    b. Encyclopedia of World History, p. 1106

CHAPTER THREE

Q.2. a. Francis M. Deng
       600 New Hampshire Avenue, NW,
       Washington, D.C. 20037
    b. Statesman's Yearbook; Statistical and
       Historical Annual of the States of the
       World, p. 1327

Q.3. a. $2,698 million
    b. Statistical Abstract of the United
       States, p. 263

Q.4. a. 1 799; 1 409 (million Naira)
    b. Statistical Yearbook, p. 710

Q.5. a. Shriver withdraws
    b. World Almanac, p. 923

Q.6. a. M. J. Neubert, Conservative
    b. Whitaker's Almanack, p. 340

CHAPTER FOUR

Q.2. a. Plate 97, War of 1812, Chesapeake
       Region
    b. Atlas of American History

Q.3. a. Historical Atlas of the United States
    b. Map no. 223, p. 146

Q.4. a. Historical Atlas
    b. p. 29, 1:6,000,000

CHAPTER FIVE

Q.2. a. Dictionary of American History, v. 6,
       pp. 374-5
    b. The Concept of Jacksonian Democracy

Q.3. a. J. H. Parry
    b. Cambridge Economic History of Europe,
       pp. 595-597

Q.4. a. G. Zeller
    b. Establishment of permanent embassies
    c. New Cambridge Modern History, v. 5

CHAPTER SIX

Q.2. a. Poland, 1867-1935
    b. Webster's Biographical Dictionary,
       p. 1185

Q.3. a. journalist
    b. Dictionary of National Biography, v. 14,
       p. 159 or v. 40, p. 159

Q.4. a. Herbert Levi Osgood, An American Scholar
    b. Dictionary of American Biography, v. 14,
       pp. 78-9

Q.5. a. Syracuse U.
    b. Directory of American Scholars, p. 471

CHAPTER SEVEN

Q.3. a. French, colonial party and French
       colonial war aims, 1914-1918.
       C. M. Andrew and A. S. Kanya-Forstner.
       Historical Journal 17:79-106 Mr '74.
    b. p. 144

Q.4. a. Del Papa, Eugene M. "The Royal
       Proclamation of 1763: Its Effect Upon
       Virginia Land Companies." Virginia
       Mag. of Hist. and Biog., 1975, 83(4):
       406-411.
    b. America: History and Life, p. 313

CHAPTER SEVEN, continued

Q.5. a. Kuper, Leo. "Theories of Revolution and
         Race Relations." <u>Comparative Studies
         in Soc. and Hist.</u>, 1971, 13(1): 87-107.
      b. p. 24

CHAPTER EIGHT

Q.2. a. Butow, Robert Joseph Charles. John
         Doe associates; backdoor diplomacy for
         peace, 1941.
      b. <u>Bibliographic Index</u>, p. 241 or 466

Q.3. a. Education in Latin America: A partial
         bibliography
      b. <u>A World Bibliography of Bibliographies
         and of Bibliographical Catalogs,
         Calendars, Abstracts, Digests, Indexes
         and the Like</u>, v. 2, c. 1848

Q.4. a. Cotton, Edward. A voice from Waterloo.
         3rd ed. reprinted. Wakefield: E. P.
         Publishing, 1974.
      b. <u>Subject Catalog; A Cumulative List of
         Works Represented by Library of
         Congress Printed Cards</u>, v. 18,
         p. 458

CHAPTER NINE

Q.2. a. Robert D. Marcus, State University of
         New York, Stony Brook
      b. "Clio With Soul"
      c. April 17, 1969, Philadelphia, Penn.
      d. J. Meredith Neil

Q.3. a. Oregon Historical Quarterly
      b. <u>Magazines for Libraries</u>, pp. 419-20

CHAPTER TEN

Q.2. a. <u>Canadian Journal of History</u>, 10:138-9,
         April 1975, D. E. Meerse.
      b. p. 807

Q.3. a. James A. Lewis
      b. Western Carolina University
      c. pp. 147-148

Q.4. a. Russell F. Weigley
      b. Temple University
      c. pp. 59-63

CHAPTER ELEVEN

Q.2. a. News-Leader
      b. 1872
      c. p. 897

Q.3. a. '70 econ rev, '71 outlook

      b. Ja 29,48:5
      c. p. 1508

Q.4. a. Aged persons--not meeting needs
      b. Aug. 20, 2a
      c. p. 153

CHAPTER TWELVE

Q.2. a. <u>Dept. of Economic and Community
         Development</u>. The State of Maryland
         historical atlas; a review of events
         and forces that have influenced the
         development of the State, prepared by
         Raymond, Parish, Pine & Plavnick.
         [Annapolis] 1973. 60 p. illus.
      b. <u>Monthly Checklist of State Publications</u>,
         p. 494

Q.3. a. Kentucky. <u>State Archives and Records
         Service</u>. Checklist of Kentucky state
         publications. 1962+ Frankfort.
         annual. OR Kentucky; monthly
         checklist of Kentucky state
         publications. Lexington University of
         Kentucky Libraries.
      b. <u>Government Publications: A Guide to
         Bibliographical Tools</u>, pp. 104-105

Q.4. a. (60) 6263
      b. German Northern theater of operations,
         1940-45. [1960.] xi+342 p.

MATERIALS & METHODS
FOR
HISTORY RESEARCH

Answer by Book

Book No. __15__

CHAPTER ONE

Q.2. a. A reference guide to English, American,
        and Canadian literature; an annotated
        checklist of bibliographical and other
        reference materials
     b. Guide to Reference Books, p. 323

Q.3. a. The West Point Atlas of American Wars
     b. The Historian's Handbook: A Descriptive
        Guide to Reference Works, p. 141

Q.4. a. Phases in the religion of ancient Rome
     b. Guide to Historical Literature, p.163

Q.5. a. Fear, War, and the Bomb
     b. Harvard Guide to American History,
        p. 1026

CHAPTER TWO

Q.2. a. $271,259,599 (in $1,000)
     b. Historical Statistics of the United
        States; Colonial Times to 1970,
        p. 1117

Q.3. a. Webb-Kenyon Interstate Liquor Act
     b. Encyclopedia of American History, p. 326

Q.4. a. Treaty of Schönbrunn
     b. Encyclopedia of World History, p. 644

CHAPTER THREE

Q.2. a. Telesphore Yaguibou
        5500 16th St., NW,
        Washington, D.C. 20011
     b. Statesman's Yearbook; Statistical and
        Historical Annual of the States of the
        World, p. 1454

Q.3. a. $575 million
     b. Statistical Abstract of the United
        States, p. 263

Q.4. a. 15 120; 17 691 (million Guaranies)
     b. Statistical Yearbook, p. 710

Q.5. a. Jackson wins New York primary; Carter
        beats Udall and Ford defeats Reagan in
        Wisconsin
     b. World Almanac, p. 927

Q.6. a. J. M. Fox, Conservative
     b. Whitaker's Almanack, p. 341

CHAPTER FOUR

Q.2. a. Plate 140, Red River Region, 1865-
        1885
     b. Atlas of American History

Q.3. a. Historical Atlas of the United States
     b. Map no. 224, p. 147

Q.4. a. Historical Atlas
     b. p. 13, 1:6,000,000

CHAPTER FIVE

Q.2. a. Dictionary of American History, v. 5,
        p. 155
     b. American Communities

Q.3. a. G. B. Masefield
     b. Cambridge Economic History of Europe,
        pp. 601-602

Q.4. a. R. A. Humphreys
     b. The French in the Peninsula (1807-8)
     c. New Cambridge Modern History, v. 9

CHAPTER SIX

Q.2. a. Denmark, 1787-1832
     b. Webster's Biographical Dictionary,
        p. 1237

Q.3. a. politician
     b. Dictionary of National Biography, v. 15,
        p. 1153 or v. 45, p. 267

Q.4. a. The Richmond Family
     b. Dictionary of American Biography, v. 15,
        pp. 582-3

Q.5. a. Washington State U.
     b. Directory of American Scholars, p. 490

CHAPTER SEVEN

Q.3. a. Lloyd George and the 1918 Irish
        conscription crisis. A. J. Ward.
     b. p. 144

Q.4. a. Parker, Mary Ann. "The Elusive Meridan."
        Chronicles of Oklahoma, 1973, 51(2):
        150-158.
     b. America: History and Life, p. 280

CHAPTER SEVEN, continued

Q.5. a. Kimmerling, Baruch. Subsistence Crops,
       Cash Crops, and Urbanization: Some
       Materials from Ghana, Uganda, and the
       Ivory Coast." Rural Sociol., 1971,
       36(4): 471-487.
    b. p. 258

CHAPTER EIGHT

Q.2. a. Tulchin, Joseph S. Aftermath of war;
       World war I and U.S. policy toward
       Latin Ameria.
    b. Bibliographic Index, p. 256 or 466

Q.3. a. David Clark Cabeen. Montesquieu: a
       bibliography.
    b. A World of Bibliography of Bibliographies
       and of Bibliographical Catalogs,
       Calendars, Abstracts, Digests, Indexes
       and the Like, v. 3, c. 4011

Q.4. a. Warner, Oliver. Nelson's battles. New
       York, Macmillan, 1965.
    b. Subject Catalog; A Cumulative List of
       Works Represented by Library of
       Congress Printed Cards, v. 28, p. 418

CHAPTER NINE

Q.2. a. Lawrence S. Kaplan, Kent State
       University
    b. "John Powers and the Italians: Politics
       in a Chicago Ward, 1896-1921"
    c. 1945
    d. William Nisbet Chambers

Q.3. a. Pennsylvania History
    b. Magazines for Libraries, p. 420

CHAPTER TEN

Q.2. a. Civil War History, 21:84-5, March 1975,
       M. R. Greco.
    b. p. 846

Q.3. a. Edward D. Fitchen
    b. Brevard College
    c. pp. 255-256

Q.4. a. Edward Pessen
    b. Baruch College and The Graduate Center,
       The City University of New York
    c. pp. 222-229

CHAPTER ELEVEN

Q.2. a. Enterprise
    b. 1859
    c. p. 904

Q.3. a. '70 econ rev, '71 outlook
    b. Ja 29,55:5
    c. p. 441

Q.4. Administration--B.M.A. calls for more
       consultation
    b. July 20, 3c
    c. p. 147

CHAPTER TWELVE

Q.2. a. Division of State Parks. A plan for
       historical preservation in Nevada.
       Vol. 3. Annual preservation program.
       3d; 1973/74. [Carson City] 28 l.
       illus.
    b. Monthly Checklist of State Publications,
       p. 332

Q.3. a. Louisiana. Dept. of State. Official
       publications. v. 1+ 1935/48+ [Baton
       Rouge]. OR Public documents [of the]
       state of Louisiana. no. 1+ Feb. 1949+
       [Baton Rouge] semi-annual.
    b. Government Publications: A Guide to
       Bibliographical Tools, p. 106

Q.4. a. (56) 305
    b. Historical Study: Effects of climate on
       combat in European Russia; February
       1952. [1952.] v+81 p.

MATERIALS & METHODS
FOR
HISTORY RESEARCH

Answer by Book

Book No. __16__

CHAPTER ONE

Q.2. a. Research and reference guide to French
        studies
     b. Guide to Reference Books, p. 348

Q.3. a. Atlas of the Classical World
     b. The Historian's Handbook: A Descriptive
        Guide to Reference Works, p. 143

Q.4. a. An Economic survey of ancient Rome
     b. Guide to Historical Literature, p. 160

Q.5. a. Politics and Policies of the Truman
        Administration
     b. Harvard Guide to American History,
        p. 1032

CHAPTER TWO

Q.2. a. $274,374,223 (in $1,000)
     b. Historical Statistics of the United
        States; Colonial Times to 1970,
        p. 1117

Q.3. a. Federal Bankruptcy Act
     b. Encyclopedia of American History, p. 317

Q.4. a. Willy Brandt
     b. Encyclopedia of World History, p. 1198

CHAPTER THREE

Q.2. a. José Perez Caldas
        1918 F Street, NW,
        Washington, D.C. 20006
     b. Statesman's Yearbook; Statistical and
        Historical Annual of the States of the
        World, p. 1459

Q.3. a. $911 million
     b. Statistical Abstract of the United
        States, p. 263

Q.4. a. 1 573; 662 (000 million Pesetas)
     b. Statistical Yearbook, p. 711

Q.5. a. Carter wins Pennsylvania primary
     b. World Almanac, p. 927

Q.6. a. W. S. Churchill, Conservative
     b. Whitaker's Almanack, p. 342

CHAPTER FOUR

Q.2. a. Plate 145, The Northwest, 1865-1890
     b. Atlas of American History

Q.3. a. Historical Atlas of the United States
     b. Map no. 225, p. 147

Q.4. a. Historical Atlas
     b. p. 13, 1:6,000,000

CHAPTER FIVE

Q.2. a. Dictionary of American History, v. 5,
        p. 318
     b. History of the Pious Fund of California

Q.3. a. E. L. J. Coornaert
     b. Cambridge Economic History of Europe,
        pp. 597-601

Q.4. a. D. Dakin
     b. Contemporary acceptance of monarchical
        absolutism under the ancient regime
     c. New Cambridge Modern History, v. 8

CHAPTER SIX

Q.2. a. France, 1804-1876
     b. Webster's Biographical Dictionary,
        p. 1307

Q.3. a. soldier
     b. Dictionary of National Biography, v. 16,
        p. 349 or v. 46, p. 349

Q.4. a. Life and Correspondence of Joseph Reed
     b. Dictionary of American Biography, v. 16,
        p. 406

Q.5. a. Columbia U.
     b. Directory of American Scholars, p. 540

CHAPTER SEVEN

Q.3. a. Effects of the pony express and the
        transcontinental telegraph upon
        selected California newspapers. A. C.
        Carey. Journalism Quarterly 51:320-3
        Summ '74
     b. p. 367

Q.4. a. Carter, Gregg Lee. "Social Demography
        of the Chinese in Nevada: 1870-1880."
        Nevada Hist. Soc. Q., 1975, 18(2):
        72-89.
     b. America: History and Life, p. 294

CHAPTER SEVEN, continued

Q.5. a. Unsigned. "Government Ideologies in
         Tanzania and Zambia." Current Notes
         on Internat. Affairs, 1970, 41(12):
         613-618.
      b. p. 269

CHAPTER EIGHT

Q.2. a. Davis, Lynn Etheridge. Cold war
         begins; Soviet-Am. conflict over
         Eastern Europe.
      b. Bibliographic Index, p. 397 or 466

Q.3. a. D. B. Robertson. Reinhold Niebuhr's
         works. A bibliography.
      b. A World Bibliography of Bibliographies
         and of Bibliographical Catalogs,
         Calendars, Abstracts, Digests, Indexes
         and the Like, v. 3, c. 4245

Q.4. a. Barclay, Cyril Nelson. Battle 1066.
         London, Dent, 1966.
      b. Subject Catalog; A Cumulative List of
         Works Represented by Library of
         Congress Printed Cards, v. 18,
         p. 436

CHAPTER NINE

Q.2. a. Mark H. Haller, Temple University
      b. "A Failure of Ambassadorial Diplomacy"
      c. Sir Cecil Spring Rice
      d. Ira D. Gruber

Q.3. a. Rhode Island History
      b. Magazines for Libraries, p. 420

CHAPTER TEN

Q.2. a. Journal of American History, 62:402-3,
         September 1975, R. A. Gerber.
      b. p. 939

Q.3. a. Edward B. Jones
      b. Furman University
      c. p. 11

Q.4. a. Lawrence S. Kaplan
      b. Kent State University
      c. pp. 385-390

CHAPTER ELEVEN

Q.2. a. Bayfield County Press
      b. 1870
      c. p. 898

Q.3. a. Mali acceptance of aid from US, USSR and
         Communist China discussed as part of
         its new policy of trying to maintain
         friendship with East and West; illus.
      b. Je 20,2:3
      c. p. 961

Q.4. a. Administration--integrated service may
         offer new careers for doctors; Hunter
         report published
      b. May 31, 3a
      c. p. 147

CHAPTER TWELVE

Q.2. a. State Dept. of Archives and History.
         Visit land of beginnings; the North
         Carolina Museum of History and State
         historic sites. [Raleigh, n.d.]
         folder. illus.
      b. Monthly Checklist of State Publications,
         p. 56

Q.3. a. Maine. State Library. Augusta.
         Checklist of state of Maine
         publications received by the Maine
         State Library. 1941-44+ [Augusta]
         quarterly.
      b. Government Publications: A Guide to
         Bibliographical Tools, p. 107

Q.4. a. (69) 16071
      b. United States Army in World War II:
         Mediterranean theater of operations
         [v. 3] Salerna to Cassino. 1969.
         xvii+491 p.

MATERIALS & METHODS
FOR
HISTORY RESEARCH

Answer by Book

Book No. ___17___

CHAPTER ONE

Q.2. a. The use of biological literature
     b. Guide to Reference Books, p. 718

Q.3. a. Penguin Atlas of Medieval History
     b. The Historian's Handbook: A Descriptive
        Guide to Reference Works, pp. 143-144

Q.4. a. Literary history of Rome from the
        origins to the close of the golden age
     b. Guide to Historical Literature, p. 162

Q.5. a. Firsthand Report: Eisenhower
        Administration
     b. Harvard Guide to American History,
        p. 1039

CHAPTER TWO

Q.2. a. $272,750,814 (in $1,000)
     b. Historical Statistics of the United
        States; Colonial Times to 1970,
        p. 1117

Q.3. a. Erdman Act
     b. Encyclopedia of American History, p. 317

Q.4. a. Dmitri T. Shepilov
     b. Encyclopedia of World History, p. 1217

CHAPTER THREE

Q.2. a. Melih Esenbel
        1606 23rd Street, NW,
        Washington, D.C. 20008
     b. Statesman's Yearbook; Statistical and
        Historical Annual of the States of the
        World, p. 1382

Q.3. a. $294 million
     b. Statistical Abstract of the United
        States, p. 263

Q.4. a. 219.7; 147.0 (million Pounds)
     b. Statistical Yearbook, p. 711

Q.5. a. Reagan beats Ford, Church beats Carter
        in Nebraska; in West Virginia, Ford
        beats Reagan, Byrd beats Wallace; in
        Connecticut Carter beats Udall
     b. World Almanac, p. 930

Q.6. a. R. J. Maxwell-Hyslop, Conservative
     b. Whitaker's Almanack, p. 343

CHAPTER FOUR

Q.2. a. Plate 123, Virginia, 1861
     b. Atlas of American History

Q.3. a. Historical Atlas of the United States
     b. Map no. 99, p. 68

Q.4. a. Historical Atlas
     b. p. 17, 1:6,000,000

CHAPTER FIVE

Q.2. a. Dictionary of American History, v. 7,
        p. 221
     b. History of Washington, Montana and Idaho

Q.3. a. L. Girard
     b. Cambridge Economic History of Europe,
        pp. 940-943

Q.4. a. Llewelyn Woodward
     b. Hitler exaggerated faults of earlier
        régimes
     c. New Cambridge Modern History, v. 12

CHAPTER SIX

Q.2. a. France, 1843-1904
     b. Webster's Biographical Dictionary,
        p. 1446

Q.3. a. ambassador
     b. Dictionary of National Biography, v. 17,
        p. 89 or v. 49, p. 89

Q.4. a. Hist. of Montgomery County, Pa.
     b. Dictionary of American Biography, v. 17,
        pp. 189-90

Q.5. a. Ohio State U.
     b. Directory of American Scholars, p. 574

CHAPTER SEVEN

Q.3. a. Beyond the Finzi-Contini garden;
        Mussolini's fascist racism. M. Van
        Creveld. Encounter 42:42-7 F '74.
     b. p. 150

Q.4. a. Berthrong, Donald J. "White Neighbors
        Come Among the Southern Cheyenne and
        Arapaho." Kansas Q., 1971, 3(4):
        105-115.
     b. America: History and Life, p. 4

CHAPTER SEVEN, continued

Q.5. a. Blackwell, James E. "Race and Crime in
Tanzania." _Phylon_, 1971, 32(2):
207-214.
b. p. 270

CHAPTER EIGHT

Q.2. a. Howard, Harry Nicholas. Turkey, the
straits and U.S. policy.
b. _Bibliographic Index_, p. 462 or 466

Q.3. a. Mary Kirk Spence. William Penn: a
bibliography. A tentative list of
publications about him and his work.
b. _A World Bibliography of Bibliographies
and of Bibliographical Catalogs,
Calendars, Abstracts, Digests, Indexes
and the Like_, v. 3, c. 4466

Q.4. a. Tetlow, Edwin. The enigma of Hastings.
London, P. Owen, 1974.
b. _Subject Catalog; A Cumulative List of
Works Represented by Library of
Congress Printed Cards_, v. 8, p. 52

CHAPTER NINE

Q.2. a. Clifford W. Trow, Oregon State
University
b. "The Welles Mission to Europe, February-
March 1940: Illusion or Realism?"
c. 1952
d. Vincent P. Carosso

Q.3. a. Texas Historian (Formerly: Junior
Historian)
b. _Magazines for Libraries_, p. 421

CHAPTER TEN

Q.2. a. _Civil War History_, 21:179-81, June
1975, E. J. Doyle.
b. p. 950

Q.3. a. Donald E. Worcester
b. Texas Christian University
c. pp. 39-40

Q.4. a. Gordon Morris Bakken
b. California State University, Fullerton
c. pp. 268-271

CHAPTER ELEVEN

Q.2. a. Independent-Register
b. 1861
c. p. 899

Q.3. a. '70 econ rev; '71 outlook; illus.
b. Ja 29,64:1
c. p. 2025

Q.4. a. Administration--report suggests training
arrangements for top-level management
are inadequate
b. Apr. 30, 4b
c. p. 151

CHAPTER TWELVE

Q.2. a. _Office of the Governor_. Regional
historic sites survey and development
plan [by] the South Texas Development
Council. [Austin] 1973. 70 p.
illus.
b. _Monthly Checklist of State Publications_,
p. 352

Q.3. a. Massachusetts. State Library, Boston.
Commonwealth of Massachusetts
publications received. [Feb. 1962+]
Boston. monthly. OR Massachusetts
Executive Department publications,
1962-1966. [Boston, 1968] 77 1.
b. _Government Publications: A Guide to
Bibliographical Tools_, p. 110

Q.4. a. (61) 5285
b. Pacific command; study in interservice
relations; 1961. [6]+29+[4] p.

MATERIALS & METHODS
FOR
HISTORY RESEARCH

Answer by Book

Book No.   18

CHAPTER ONE

Q.2. a. Guide to the bibliographies of
        Russian literature
     b. Guide to Reference Books, p. 365

Q.3. a. New York Times Index
     b. The Historian's Handbook: A Descriptive
        Guide to Reference Works, pp. 125-26.

Q.4. a. The Greek city and its institutions
     b. Guide to Historical Literature, p. 133

Q.5. a. Kennedy and the New Frontier
     b. Harvard Guide to American History,
        p. 1041

CHAPTER TWO

Q.2. a. $270,527,172 (in $1,000)
     b. Historical Statistics of the United
        States; Colonial Times to 1970,
        p. 1117

Q.3. a. Expedition Act
     b. Encyclopedia of American History, p. 319

Q.4. a. Vostok I
     b. Encyclopedia of World History, p. 1217
        or 1357

CHAPTER THREE

Q.2. a. Kokou Kekeh
        2208 Massachusetts Avenue, NW,
        Washington, D.C. 20008
     b. Statesman's Yearbook; Statistical and
        Historical Annual of the States of the
        World, p. 1369

Q.3. a. $1,004 million
     b. Statistical Abstract of the United
        States, p. 263

Q.4. a. 25 084; 9 088 (million CFA francs)
     b. Statistical Yearbook, p. 711

Q.5. a. Fred Harris quits
     b. World Almanac, p. 927

Q.6. a. J. A. Cunningham, Labour
     b. Whitaker's Almanack, p. 344

CHAPTER FOUR

Q.2. a. Plate 111, Wisconsin, Iowa and
        Minnesota Territories, 1832-1858
     b. Atlas of American History

Q.3. a. Historical Atlas of the United States
     b. Map no. 100, p. 68

Q.4. a. Historical Atlas
     b. p. 17, 1:7,500,000

CHAPTER FIVE

Q.2. a. Dictionary of American History, v. 7,
        p. 308
     b. The Wisconsin Idea

Q.3. a. A. J. Youngson
     b. Cambridge Economic History of Europe,
        pp. 938-939

Q.4. a. Rohan Butler
     b. Armistice, 11 Nov. 1918
     c. New Cambridge Modern History, v. 12

CHAPTER SIX

Q.2. a. Argentina, 1868-1932
     b. Webster's Biographical Dictionary,
        p. 1503

Q.3. a. soldier
     b. Dictionary of National Biography, v. 18,
        p. 353 or v. 52, p. 353

Q.4. a. Reuben Gold Thwaites, a Memorial Address
     b. Dictionary of American Biography, v. 18,
        pp. 521-2

Q.5. a. Harvard
     b. Directory of American Scholars, p. 633

CHAPTER SEVEN

Q.3. a. Great Britain, France, and the
        Ethiopian crisis 1935-1936. R. A. C.
        Parker. English Historical Review 89:
        293-332 Ap '74.
     b. p. 228

Q.4. a. Norwood, Frederick A. "Strangers in a
        Strange Land: Removal of the Wyandot
        Indians." Methodist Hist., 1975,
        13(3): 45-60.
     b. America: History and Life, p. 182

CHAPTER SEVEN, continued

Q.5. a. Kagombe, Maina. "Kikuyu Studies: A Case
of Conflict and Violence." Pan
African J., 1970, 3(1): 3-13.
b. p. 41

CHAPTER EIGHT

Q.2. a. Iriye, Akira. Cold war in Asia: a
hist. introduction.
b. Bibliographic Index, p. 27 or 429

Q.3. a. Robert Bartlett Haas and Donald Clifford
Gallup. A catalogue of the published
and unpublished writings of Gertrude
Stein exhibited in the Yale university
library.
b. A World Bibliography of Bibliographies
and of Bibliographical Catalogs,
Calendars, Abstracts, Digests, Indexes
and the Like, v. 4, c. 5906

Q.4. a. Blond, Georges. The Marne. Harrisburg,
Pa. 1966
b. Subject Catalog; A Cumulative List of
Works Represented by Library of
Congress Printed Cards, v. 57, p. 604

CHAPTER NINE

Q.2. a. A. E. Keir Nash, University of
California, Santa Barbara
b. "Racial Militancy and Interracial
Violence in the Second World War"
c. 1959
d. Frank L. Klement

Q.3. a. Vermont History
b. Magazines for Libraries, p. 421

CHAPTER TEN

Q.2. a. Civil War History, 21:274-6, September
1975, R. W. Johannsen.
b. p. 966

Q.3. a. Larry R. Gerlach
b. University of Utah
c. p. 61

Q.4. a. Harry Ammon
b. Southern Illinois University
c. pp. 391-396

CHAPTER ELEVEN

Q.2. a. Enterprise
b. 1875
c. p. 911

Q.3. a. Belgian Congo changes name to Zaire
Repub; new name is taken from original
name of Congo River, which in Zaire
will be called Zaire River
b. O 28,2:4
c. p. 2025

Q.4. a. Administrative staff--NALGO members
work-to-rule for shorter hours
b. Dec. 3, 4a
c. p. 158

CHAPTER TWELVE

Q.2. a. Historic Preservation Commission. The
national register of historic places
in Maine, compiled and drawn by
Richard D. Kelly. [Augusta] 1973.
map on sheet 95x55 cm.
b. Monthly Checklist of State Publications,
p. 262

Q.3. a. Minnesota. State Library. St. Paul.
Checklist. no. 1+ Aug. 1946+ St. Paul.
annual. OR Minnesota state documents.
[v. 1, no. 1+ Jan./Mar. 1970+]
St. Paul, Minnesota Historical Society
Library. quarterly. OR Minnesota
state publications. v. 1, no. 1+
July/Sept. 1957+ St. Paul, Department
of Administration. Documents Section.
irregular.
b. Government Publications: A Guide to
Bibliographical Tools, p. 113

Q.4. a. (49) 1566
b. Bougainville and Northern Solomons.
1948. vi+166 p.

MATERIALS & METHODS
FOR
HISTORY RESEARCH

Answer by Book

Book No. __19__

CHAPTER ONE

Q.2. a. Manual of Hispanic bibliography
b. Guide to Reference Books, p. 358

Q.3. a. Who's Who in Latin America
b. The Historian's Handbook: A Descriptive
Guide to Reference Works, p. 167

Q.4. a. Food in early Greece
b. Guide to Historical Literature, p. 135

Q.5. a. American Foreign Policy and the Cold War
b. Harvard Guide to American History,
p. 1046

CHAPTER TWO

Q.2. a. $276,343,218 (in $1,000)
b. Historical Statistics of the United
States; Colonial Times to 1970,
p. 1117

Q.3. a. National Defense Act
b. Encyclopedia of American History, p. 328

Q.4. a. 1889-1914
b. Encyclopedia of World History, p. 593

CHAPTER THREE

Q.2. a. Anand Panyarachun
2300 Kalorama Rd., NW,
Washington, D.C. 20008
b. Statesman's Yearbook; Statistical and
Historical Annual of the States of the
World, p. 1367

Q.3. a. $551 million
b. Statistical Abstract of the United
States, p. 263

Q.4. a. 28.75; 22.74 (000 million Kroner)
b. Statistical Yearbook, p. 711

Q.5. a. Reagan beat Ford in Texas
b. World Almanac, p. 930

Q.6. a. C. G. D. Onslow, Conservative
b. Whitaker's Almanack, p. 344

CHAPTER FOUR

Q.2. a. Plate 131, Trans-Mississippi, 1861-
1865
b. Atlas of American History

Q.3. a. Historical Atlas of the United States
b. Map no. 214, p. 142

Q.4. a. Historical Atlas
b. p. 33, 1:25,000,000

CHAPTER FIVE

Q.2. a. Dictionary of American History, v. 4,
p. 83
b. Legion of the Lafayette

Q.3. a. A. Gerschenkron
b. Cambridge Economic History of Europe,
pp. 1014-1017

Q.4. a. R. E. Robinson and J. Gallagher
b. The nature of imperialism in Africa
c. New Cambridge Modern History, v. 11

CHAPTER SIX

Q.2. a. Germany, 1808-1888
b. Webster's Biographical Dictionary,
p. 1552

Q.3. a. physician
b. Dictionary of National Biography, v. 19,
p. 246 or v. 55, p. 246

Q.4. a. Israel, Elihu and Cadwallader Washburn
b. Dictionary of American Biography, v. 19,
pp. 502-3

Q.5. a. U. of Chicago
b. Directory of American Scholars, p. 649

CHAPTER SEVEN

Q.3. a. Blouse and the frock coat: the alliance
of the common people of Paris with the
liberal leadership and the middle
class during the last years of the
Bourbon restoration. E. L. Newman.
Journal of Modern History. 46:26-59
Mr '74.
b. p. 161

Q.4. a. Francaviglia, Richard V. "Some Comments
on the Historic and Geographic
Importance of Railroads in Minnesota."
Minnesota Hist., 1972, 43(2): 58-62.
b. America: History and Life, p. 154

CHAPTER SEVEN, continued

Q.5. a. Calamitsis, Evangelos A. "Stabilization
       Problems and Policies in Tunisia."
       Finance and Development. 1970, 7(3):
       43-48.
     b. p. 44

CHAPTER EIGHT

Q.2. a. McCann, Frank D. Brazilian-American
       alliance, 1937-1945.
     b. Bibliographic Index, p. 52 or 429

Q.3. a. Burt Franklin and George Legman. David
       Ricardo and ricardian theory. A
       bibliographical checklist.
     b. A World Bibliography of Bibliographies
       and of Bibliographical Catalogs,
       Calendars, Abstracts, Digests, Indexes
       and the Like, v. 4, c. 5395.

Q.4. a. Brown, Wilburt S. The amphibious
       campaign for West Florida and
       Louisiana. 1814-1815; a cultural
       review of strategy and tactics at New
       Orleans. University, Ala., University
       of Alabama Press, 1969.
     b. Subject Catalog; A Cumulative List of
       Works Represented by Library of
       Congress Printed Cards, v. 28, p. 339

CHAPTER NINE

Q.2. a. Richard H. Kohn, Rutgers University
     b. "The New Deal and the Negro Community:
       Toward a Broader Conceptualization"
     c. Organization of American Historians'
       Pelzer Award
     d. James A. Rawley

Q.3. a. Virginia Cavalcade of Virginia Magazine
       of History and Biography
     b. Magazines for Libraries, p. 421

CHAPTER TEN

Q.2. a. Journal of American History, 62:383-5,
       September 1975, N. E. Cunningham, Jr.
     b. p. 941

Q.3. a. Norman Lederer
     b. Camden County College
     c. p. 127

Q.4. a. Howard P. Chudacoff
     b. Brown University
     c. pp. 99-104

CHAPTER ELEVEN

Q.2. a. Forest Republican
     b. 1887
     c. p. 900

Q.3. a. Copper indus nationalized
     b. Ja 2,4:3
     c. p. 2300

Q.4. a. Administration--costs to be reviewed
     b. July 2, 2d
     c. p. 176

CHAPTER TWELVE

Q.2. a. State Parks and Recreation Commission.
       Preserving heritage sites in
       Washington State. [Olympia, n.d. 6]p.
       illus.
     b. Monthly Checklist of State Publications,
       p. 70

Q.3. a. Mississippi. Public documents no. 1+
       July/Dec. 1966+ Jackson. semiannual.
       Issued by the Secretary of State.
     b. Government Publications: A Guide to
       Bibliographical Tools, p. 113

Q.4. a. (63) 5653
     b. At Close Quarters, PT boats in United
       States Navy. 1962. xxiv+574+[5] p.

MATERIALS & METHODS
FOR
HISTORY RESEARCH

Answer by Book

Book No. ___20___

CHAPTER ONE

Q.2. a. Guide to the literature of mathematics
       and physics including related works on
       engineering science
    b. Guide to Reference Books, p. 763

Q.3. a. Columbia Lippincott Gazetteer of the
       World
    b. The Historian's Handbook: A Descriptive
       Guide to Reference Works, pp. 130-131

Q.4. a. The Greek and Macedonian Art of War
    b. Guide to Historical Literature, p. 136

Q.5. a. Vietnam and American Foreign Policy
    b. Harvard Guide to American History,
       p. 1053

CHAPTER TWO

Q.2. a. $284,705,907 (in $1,000)
    b. Historical Statistics of the United
       States; Colonial Times to 1970,
       p. 1117

Q.3. a. Aldrich-Vreeland Act
    b. Encyclopedia of American History, p. 321

Q.4. a. 1867, 1885, 1895
    b. Encyclopedia of World History, p. 593

CHAPTER THREE

Q.2. a. Sabah Kabbani
       600 New Hampshire Avenue, NW,
       Washington, D.C. 20037
    b. Statesman's Yearbook; Statistical and
       Historical Annual of the States of the
       World, p. 1361

Q.3. a. $132 million
    b. Statistical Abstract of the United
       States, p. 263

Q.4. a. 265.7; 128.2 (million Kwachas)
    b. Statistical Yearbook, p. 712

Q.5. a. Reagan defeats Ford narrowly in Indiana,
       Carter wins in Indiana and Georgia,
       loses in Alabama to Wallace
    b. World Almanac, p. 930

Q.6. a. T. L. Higgins, Conservative
    b. Whitaker's Almanack, p. 345

CHAPTER FOUR

Q.2. a. Plate 143, Sioux-Cheyenne Country,
       1865-1890
    b. Atlas of American History

Q.3. a. Historical Atlas of the United States
    b. Map no. 215, p. 142

Q.4. a. Historical Atlas
    b. p. 33, 1:25,000,000

CHAPTER FIVE

Q.2. a. Dictionary of American History, v. 4,
       p. 282
    b. The Mecklenburg Declaration of
       Independence

Q.3. a. Davis S. Landes
    b. Cambridge Economic History of Europe,
       pp. 943-1007

Q.4. a. A. P. Thornton
    b. The interests and policies of the
       European powers
    c. New Cambridge Modern History, v. 11

CHAPTER SIX

Q.2. a. Germany, 1864-1940
    b. Webster's Biographical Dictionary,
       p. 1618

Q.3. a. politician
    b. Dictionary of National Biography, v. 21,
       p. 232 or v. 61, p. 232

Q.4. a. Biog. and Hist. Sketches of Early Ind.
    b. Dictionary of American Biography, v. 20,
       pp. 559-60

Q.5. a. Harvard
    b. Directory of American Scholars, p. 656

CHAPTER SEVEN

Q.3. a. Pindar and Athens: a reading in the
       Aeginetan odes. W. Mullen. Arion
       ns 1, no. 3:446-95 '73-74.
    b. p. 186

Q.4. a. Ray, Roger B., ed. "An Addendum to:
       'Maine Indians' Concept of Land
       Tenure,' MHS Quarterly, Vol. 13,
       pp. 28-51." Maine Hist. Soc. Q., 1974,
       13(3): 178-184.
    b. America: History and Life, pp. 309-310

CHAPTER SEVEN, continued

Q.5. a. Lee, J. M. "Clan Loyalties and
Socialist Doctrine in the People's
Republic of the Congo." World Today,
1971, 27(1): 40-46.
   b. p. 160

CHAPTER EIGHT

Q.2. a. Gellman, Irwin F. Roosevelt and
Batista; good neighbor diplomacy in
Cuba. 1933-1945.
   b. Bibliographic Index, p. 100 or 429

Q.3. a. Daphne W. Thomson. Cecil John Rhodes.
A bibliography.
   b. A World Bibliography of Bibliographies
and of Bibliographical Catalogs,
Calendars, Abstracts, Digests, Indexes
and the Like, v. 4, c. 5392

Q.4. a. Battle of New Orleans sesquicentennial
historical booklets. New Orleans,
Battle of New Orleans, 150th
Anniversary Committee of Louisiana,
distributed by Louisiana Landmarks
Society, New Orleans Chapter, 1965.
   b. Subject Catalog; A Cumulative List of
Works Represented by Library of
Congress Printed Cards, v. 64,
p. 451

CHAPTER NINE

Q.2. a. Gary B. Nash, University of California,
Los Angeles
   b. "The Character of the Congressional
Revolution of 1910"
   c. 1963
   d. A. P. Nasatir

Q.3. a. New York Historical Society Quarterly or
New York History or The Yorker
   b. Magazines for Libraries, p. 419, or
p. 419, or p. 421

CHAPTER TEN

Q.2. a. Journal of American History, 62:382-3,
September 1975, R. C. Carriker.
   b. p. 807

Q.3. a. Phillip D. Thomas
   b. Wichita State University
   c. p. 163

Q.4. a. William L. Barney
   b. University of North Carolina at Chapel
Hill
   c. pp. 551-557

CHAPTER ELEVEN

Q.2. a. Times
   b. 1880
   c. p. 903

Q.3. a. '69 econ rev; outlook bright despite
widespread damage from Oct floods
   b. Ja 30,56:1
   c. p. 1932

Q.4. a. Administrative structure review
announced
   b. Nov. 7, 1d
   c. p. 92

CHAPTER TWELVE

Q.2. a. Dept. of State. Division of Michigan
History. Michigan's historic
attractions. [Lansing, c1973] 31 p.
illus.
   b. Monthly Checklist of State Publications,
p. 389

Q.3. a. New Hampshire. State Library, Concord.
Checklist of New Hampshire state
departments publications. 1942/44+
[Concord] biennial.
   b. Government Publications: A Guide to
Bibliographical Tools, p. 117

Q.4. a. (54) 8594
   b. Imperial Japanese Navy in World War II,
graphic presentation of Japanese naval
organization and list of combatant and
non-combatant vessels lost or damaged
in the War; Feb. 1952. [11]+279+
[22] p.

Materials & Methods
for
History Research
Workbook

TABLE OF CONTENTS

ACKNOWLEDGEMENTS

The technique of using a manual to teach bibliographic skills was first developed by Miriam Dudley of UCLA. There is no more apt beginning for those who build upon the method than to acknowledge her work. In deciding upon the materials to include in this manual, the classification of them, and the sorts of things to say about them, the authors have benefited from close consideration of Sources of Information in the Social Sciences edited by Carl White, Literature and Bibliography of the Social Sciences by Thelma Freides, Guide to the Use of Books and Libraries by Jean Gates, and Historian's Handbook by Helen Poulton. The flow charts in Chapter Thirteen were redrawn and modified from Thomas Kirk, "Problems in Library Instruction in Four-Year Colleges" in Educating the Library User (New York: R. R. Bowker) edited by John Lubans, pages 93-95.

The development of a teaching source such as this manual requires the efforts of many people. For their assistance in the preparation of this manual, the authors are indebted to several members of the University of Wisconsin-Parkside's Library/Learning Center Staff. Among them, Lawrence Crumb, Maria Soule, Patricia Berge, Shirley Mandernack, Diane Lichter, Julie Glaeser and Christine Vlahakis deserve special thanks. The history faculty's Dr. Thomas Reeves provided encouragement as well as the course setting for developing and testing the manual. Finally, the students of four successive years in the history methods course at Parkside deserve acknowledgement. In 1974-75, they absorbed material on library skills in lecture form. The reactions of that class were reflected in the first written version of this manual, presented to the 1975-76 students. Their reactions in turn served as indicators for extensive revisions of the manual. More recently, student response in the 1976-77 and 1977-78 classes has encouraged the authors to present the manual to a wider audience.

INTRODUCTION

The ability to locate information in an organized and efficient manner is an important asset for students. The more they know about the materials and methods necessary for effective information gathering, the more productive and less time consuming they will find their research and independent study time. In addition, effective library research skills will enable students after they leave school to further their educational development through the use of information sources available in most libraries.

This manual focuses on methods of information gathering and types of information sources appropriate for research and independent study in history. The specific objectives of the manual are:

--to introduce basic types of information sources that history students should be able to use;

--to familiarize students with important examples of each type of source; and

--to prepare students to use those information sources efficiently and effectively in independent study and research.

Upon completion of the assignments in this manual, students should be able to:

--identify and use specialized historical reference sources such as guides, subject dictionaries and encyclopedias, biographical sources, indexes, abstracts, and bibliographies;

--locate articles and book reviews in historical journals;
--locate and use newspaper articles in research;
--locate and use government publications in research;
--evaluate the quality of books by using reviews or other criteria discussed in the manual;
--utilize specific research techniques and search strategies for efficient and effective information gathering;
--cite periodicals, books, and documents according to standard bibliographic form.

To put these objectives within the context of a specific example, students assigned a paper or wanting information on Franklin D. Roosevelt should, with the materials explained in this manual, be able quickly and easily to find: brief summaries of information on the major political, social, and economic problems of the period; lists of articles and books about him, his career, and the major events of his era; newspaper accounts of his public activities and statements; book reviews useful in selecting a balanced coverage of his life and accomplishments; and government publications including his presidential messages and papers.

This manual is made up of thirteen chapters and an appendix. The first chapter deals with works which introduce reference materials, research source materials, and standard studies of historical topics. Chapters Two through Six discuss content reference works; these are sources of either statistical or narrative information useful in study and research. Chapters Seven and Eight introduce finding aids; these reference works, such as indexes and bibliographies, identify scholarly studies of individual topics. In Chapter Nine, a specialized source containing scholarly studies, the historical journal, is discussed. Chapter Ten consists of a discussion of some of the means by which students can evaluate the quality of books on individual historical topics. In Chapters Eleven and Twelve, the discussion focuses on two types of source materials used by historians, newspapers and government publications, which are available to most students.

Each of these chapters discusses the organization of the sources and their utility for history students. Standard examples of each type of source are described individually. The assignments accompanying the chapters ask students to use those standard sources to locate information. Each brief assignment translates the discussion in a chapter to practical experience, demonstrating for students the ease with which sources can be located and information secured. The focus of the last chapter is on research and study techniques and strategies which bring together the various types of sources discussed in previous chapters within the context of an individual research project. The Appendix lists additional examples of each of the types of sources discussed in Chapters One through Twelve.

The intention behind this manual is not to present an exhaustive treatment of its subject matter. Rather, the bibliographic examples have been selected according to the following criteria: (1) they are all in the English language; (2) they are generally available in medium size college libraries; (3) they are important examples of the types of sources most useful to history majors.

Too often, learning bibliographic skills is an unnecessarily haphazard and time consuming process that leaves students unfamiliar with many types of sources that would increase the ease and productivity of their study hours. It is hoped that this manual will offer those who use it a more thorough and less frustrating introduction to bibliographic sources useful to the study of history.

NOTE TO THE STUDENT

In order to carry out research efficiently, you must be familiar with the library's major services and collections, its classification system for books and periodicals, and the arrangement of the card catalogue. If you have questions about these matters consult either the printed descriptive materials available in the library or a reference librarian before you begin to use this manual.

A few simple procedures, if followed as you use this manual, will maximize its benefits to you and minimize the time you spend on the exercises. Be sure to read the text material, and especially the source annotations, carefully before turning to the assignment sheet for each chapter. Read the entire assignment sheet before attempting to do any of the questions, and make a preliminary decision about which source discussed in the chapter is appropriate for each question. When using a source for the first time, examine its table of contents, explanatory material in its preface and/or introduction, and the index, if there is one, to determine how the source can most efficiently be used.

There are no "trick" questions in the assignments. If you spend more than ten to fifteen minutes on an individual question, your approach to the problem may be incorrect. Ask a reference librarian for advice. You should also seek help from a reference librarian when you cannot find a source where it should be shelved or on a nearby table in the reference area.

Finally, because each of the chapters in this manual has a very specific focus, it is important to read the Introduction carefully. Besides imparting an initial sense of the content of the manual, it should convey an idea of the overall research ability to which each of the chapters contributes.

Chapter 1

GUIDES TO THE LITERATURE

Objective 1:   After reading this chapter, the student will
               describe a situation in which a guide would be
               useful.
Objective 2:   Given a subject field other than a social science,
               the student will use a comprehensive guide to
               identify an appropriate example of a specified
               type of reference source (a guide, encyclopedia,
               bibliography, etc.).
Objective 3:   Given a topic in history, the student will select
               an appropriate guide to historical literature,
               and use it to identify a specified reference
               work.
Objective 4:   Given a topic in history, the student will select
               an appropriate guide and use it to identify a
               book-length study on the topic.

Guides to the literature introduce various types of

publications available in a given subject field or fields. The

purpose of a guide is to identify the sources that will enable

students to successfully undertake information searches on

individual topics. There are guides which focus almost exclu-

sively on the two principal categories of references works:

finding aids, such as bibliographies and periodical indexes;

and content reference works, such as handbooks, subject

dictionaries, and subject encyclopedias. Some guides include

discussions of various types of primary research materials

such as government publications. A few guides include lists

of important book-length studies, and in some cases even

journal articles, on topics in the subject field. The uses of

each of these types of publications will be discussed in

subsequent chapters of this manual.

Students unfamiliar with a subject discipline can identify
its reference publications by consulting a guide which attempts
coverage of a wide spectrum of the fields of knowledge.
The standard general guide is:

Sheehy, Eugene P. <u>Guide to Reference Books</u>. 9th ed.
Chicago: American Library Association, 1976.

    The primary purpose of this volume is to list and
evaluate reference sources. Individual books are grouped
under the headings: General Reference Works; The
Humanities; Social Sciences; History and Area Studies;
Pure and Applied Sciences. Within each group, titles are
subdivided by subject, and then by specific type of
material (encyclopedia, dictionary, bibliography, etc.).
The ninth edition lists over 10,500 titles, most of them
published before 1973, although some 1974 reference works
are included. There is an index of authors, titles, and
specific topics.

For most academic disciplines, there are specialized guides
to the literature. For a guide to the literature of history
which identifies reference and source materials, but not
historical journals, journal articles, or book-length studies
of individual topics, students may turn to:

Poulton, Helen J. <u>The Historian's Handbook: A Descriptive
Guide to Reference Works</u>. Norman: University of Oklahoma
Press, 1972.

    This work introduces several of the different types of
reference and research sources (encyclopedias, bibliographies, government publications, etc.) useful to
historians. Each chapter introduces a type, describes its
uses, and discusses individual titles. The table of
contents serves as a useful outline of the chapters. In
addition to an index of titles, there is a general index
of topics, types of material, and authors.

Of the guides to historical literature which give extensive
attention to materials other than reference sources, two are

particularly useful, the first because of its comprehensive

geographic and temporal scope, the second because of its

thorough treatment of American history. They are:

American Historical Association. Guide to Historical
Literature. New York: Macmillan, 1961.

Although somewhat out-of-date, this work remains a
useful guide to the literature of world history. The
detailed table of contents should be relied upon to locate
a section dealing with a particular region or country at a
particular time. There are separate lists of various
types of reference materials, printed source materials,
journals, and book-length studies on individual topics in
each section.

Freidel, Frank, ed. Harvard Guide to American History.
Rev. ed. Cambridge: Harvard University Press, 1974.

This extensive two-volume guide begins with a section
which explains and lists reference and source materials.
Subsequent sections in the first volume list journal
articles and monographs (book-length studies) in broad
topical categories such as economic history, immigration
and ethnicity, politics, etc. In the second volume,
articles and monographs are listed in sections on specific
periods of American history.

Chapter 1

GUIDES TO THE LITERATURE

Assignment

1. Describe a situation in which you as a history student
    would use a guide to the literature.

2. You are taking_____
    _____
    and the instructor has asked each student to select an
    independent study project. You feel that in defining your
    project you should consult specialized reference books. To
    identify a guide to these books, you consult a general
    guide to reference books.

    a. What is the title of the first English language guide
        listed for your subject field? (Use the index to
        locate the correct title.)

    b. In which source and on what page did you find the title?

3. Your instructor is conducting your resources and methods
    in history course in the library for several class
    periods to familiarize the students with basic reference
    sources. The instructor has asked each student to report
    on how a particular type of reference source can be used in
    historical research, and to use an individual title as an
    example of the type. For your report you will be using

    _____
    _____.
    For individual titles you consult the guide to historical
    literature discussed in this chapter which treats only
    reference and research sources.

    a. What is the first English language title given which
        meets your requirements?

    b. In which source and on what page(s) did you find this
        title discussed?

4. In your course on_____

each student has been assigned a special topic for independent study. You have been asked to do your reading on

_____

_____

and to write a paper on some aspect of that topic. As a
first step, you consult a guide to historical literature
discussed in this chapter for titles of book-length studies
on your topic.

   a. What is the first English language title listed on your
       topic?

   b. In which source and on what page did you find this
       information?

5. In conjunction with a series of lectures on_____

_____,
the professor in your American history survey course asks
you to select a book on_____

_____
_____for a class report.
For a list of titles on that topic, you consult the guide
discussed in this chapter which extensively surveys the
literature of American history.

   a. What is the first title listed in the section
       appropriate to your topic?

   b. In which source and on what page did you find this
       information?

Chapter 2

HANDBOOKS

Objective 1: After reading this chapter, the student will describe a situation in which a history student would use a handbook.

Objective 2: Given a subject, the student will locate statistical information using a handbook discussed in this chapter.

Objective 3: Given an event or date, the student will use a handbook discussed in this chapter to locate specified information.

A handbook is a compact fact book designed for quick reference. Usually a handbook deals with one broad subject area, and it emphasizes generally accepted data rather than recent findings. In the latter respect, handbooks differ from yearbooks, discussed in Chapter Three, although these reference tools overlap in the types of information they include and in their utility for researchers.

Among the handbooks useful for historians are those which provide information in statistical form on matters such as demographic trends, economic developments, elections, and so on. Gathered from several sources, the statistics conveniently available in a reliable handbook provide data necessary for precise descriptions and/or analysis of historical trends, developments, and events. Among the statistical handbooks useful to history majors is:

Historical Statistics of the United States: Colonial Times to 1970. Washington, D.C.: Government Printing Office, 1975.

This two-volume work contains statistics on a wide
spectrum of social and economic developments from the
colonial period to the present. The tables are accompanied by explanatory notes and references to additional
sources of statistical information. To use this work
effectively, the student may turn to the table of contents
which provides a broad subject access; the subject index
which offers a more narrow topical approach to the data;
or the time period index which provides access to
statistics on major topics for individual decades.

Chronological compendia, a second type of handbook, list,

and in most cases briefly describe, historical events. Although

they neither analyze nor explain those events, chronological

compendia can serve students as versatile introductory sources

of information. For example, students may turn to compendia

for summaries of treaties and important laws, to identify the

major events that preceded or followed a particular occurrence,

or for comparative lists of events in different countries at a

particular time. Examples of chronological compendia include:

Morris, Richard B. and Jeffrey B. Morris. Encyclopedia of
American History. New York: Harper & Row, 1976.

   This source covers American historical events from
   the era of discovery and exploration to 1974. Part one
   is a basic chronology of the major political and military
   events in American history. Part two is a topical
   chronology of constitutional development, American
   expansion, and demographic, economic, scientific, and
   cultural developments. Part three consists of
   biographical sketches of five hundred notable Americans.
   The detailed subject index provides access to
   information for which students have no time frame.

Langer, William. Encyclopedia of World History. 5th
ed. Boston: Houghton Mifflin, 1972.

   This telescoped narrative of historical material,
   chronologically arranged, deals mainly with political,
   military, and diplomatic events for most periods of
   history and regions of the world. Outline maps and
   genealogical tables are scattered through the text. The
   index is detailed and is an excellent device for quickly
   locating information about specific events.

Chapter 2

HANDBOOKS

Assignment

1. Describe a situation in which a history student would use a
    handbook.

2. In one of your readings on recent American history, the
    author uses the increase in the federal public debt to
    support a point. He makes a statement about the debt in
    _____.
    You decide to check his figures.

    a. What was the federal <u>public</u> debt in that year?

    b. In which source and on what page did you find this
        information?

3. In your American history survey course, the instructor has
    given each student a list of dates, and has asked for
    information on their historical significance. One of your
    dates is_____.

    a. What happened on that date? (You need only supply the
        information presented in bold print in the source you
        consult.)

    b. In which source and on what page did you find this
        information?

4. In your western civilization course, each student has been asked to find answers to questions on an assigned topic. Your topic is:_____

    _____ .

    a. One of your questions is:_____

        _____
        _____
        _____?

    b. In which source and on what page(s) did you find this information?

Chapter 3

YEARBOOKS AND ALMANACS

Objective 1:   After reading this chapter, the student will
               describe a situation in which a yearbook or
               almanac would be an appropriate source of informa-
               tion in historical research.
Objective 2:   Given a subject and year, the student will use an
               appropriate yearbook to locate specified data.
Objective 3:   Given a subject and country, the student will use
               an almanac to locate specified information about
               the subject.

While yearbooks often contain a good deal of background

information, they are essentially fact books which focus on the

developments and events of a given year. Unlike handbooks,

they emphasize current information. Like handbooks, yearbooks

may present only statistics, information in narrative form, or

a combination of the two. History students may use current or

back issues of reliable yearbooks for statistical information

and/or narrative information on major political, social and

economic developments. Among the most reliable yearbooks are:

Statesman's Yearbook: Statistical and Historical Annual
of the States of the World. New York: St. Martin's
Press, 1864-.

   Combines information from official and unofficial
sources on all countries of the world. It is divided
into four major parts: international organizations, the
British Commonwealth, the United States, and the rest of
the world. For each country there is information on its
history, constitution and government, economy, area and
population, religion, diplomatic representatives, etc. To
locate information on a particular country, use the "Place
and International Organizations Index."

Statistical Abstract of the United States. Washington,
D.C.: Government Printing Office, 1878-.

A recognized and reliable source for statistics on
American society, politics, and the economy. Emphasis is
on information of national scope but there are also tables
for regions, individual states, the Commonwealth of Puerto
Rico, and other outlying areas of the United States. To
locate statistics on a specific topic, researchers may use
the subject index; for statistics on more broad subjects,
the table of contents is more useful. The introductory
text to each section, the source notes for each table, and
the bibliography of sources are useful guides to other
statistical sources.

United Nations. Statistical Office. Statistical Yearbook.
New York: 1949-.

This annual publication contains information on
all countries, with statistical tables on population,
agriculture, industry, consumption, transportation,
external trade, wages and prices, national income,
finance, education, etc. Normally a ten- to 20-year
span is covered in each statistical series. The table
of contents provides the only subject access. The
original sources of the statistics are cited. Textual
material, including indexes, is in French and English.

Almanacs are also annual compendia of statistics and/or

information in narrative form. A basic difference between

yearbooks and almanacs lies in the superficiality of treatment

usually afforded important developments in almanacs. This is a

reflection of the specific purpose of the almanac, which is to

present information about an exceptionally broad range of

subjects. Among the best almanacs are:

World Almanac. New York: Newspaper Enterprise Association,
1868-.

The most detailed and comprehensive almanac published
in the United States, the World Almanac contains information on social, industrial, political, financial,
religious, educational and other developments. Each
country is treated in a separate section, with the United
States receiving the most extensive coverage. The review

of the top political and news events of the year is useful. The subject index is fairly extensive and is located at the beginning of the volume.

Whitaker's Almanack. London: J. Whitaker and Sons, Ltd., 1869-.

This is the British counterpart of the World Almanac. It is issued in three editions: the complete edition with maps, the complete edition without maps, and the short edition. All editions review political, economic, and social developments in the United Kingdom for the year. The complete editions include information about the Commonwealth countries, the United States, and the United Nations, and review the year in science, literature, and art. All editions contain a subject index which is located at the front of each volume.

Although both yearbooks and almanacs are useful sources of information, a distinction should be observed regarding their utility in the preparation of written reports. Reliable yearbooks are credible sources for citation in research papers when a more original source is not available. (For example, a table in Statistical Abstract of the United States citing statistics from the 1970 Census of Population may be used if the census volume is not available.) On the other hand, the nature and purpose of almanacs render them inappropriate for citation in most cases. Students should turn to more specialized sources, often identified in the almanacs, for acceptable citations.

Chapter 3

YEARBOOKS AND ALMANACS

Assignment

1. Describe a situation in which a yearbook or almanac would
    be an appropriate source of information in historical
    research.

2. In your course on the world in the twentieth century,
    your instructor has asked each student to select a topic
    for a research paper. In collecting data for your paper
    on _____, you decide to write to its
    ambassador in the United States to see if the embassy has
    any official publications which contain the information
    you need.

    a. What is the name and address of that country's
        ambassador to the United States? (Use the 1976/77
        edition of a source discussed in this chapter.)

    b. In which source and on what page did you find this
        information?

3. Recently, President Carter stated that a disproportionate amount of federal aid to state and local governments goes to "Sun Belt" states. As a research project for your seminar on the history of the United States since World War II, you have decided to study trends in federal aid to the states during the 1960s and 1970s.

    a. What was the total federal aid to_____ for 1975? (Use the 1976 edition of a source discussed in this chapter.)

    b. In which source and on what page did you find this information?

4. In her lectures on contemporary trends, your instructor in twentieth century economic history cites the expansion of the monetary supply of most countries in the 1970s to support statements she makes about world economic conditions. For a class report, she asks you to test her assertion in relation to the_____ countries by collecting statistics on the expansion of the monetary supply in each of them from 1970 to 1974. Using a source discussed in this chapter,

    a. What are summary figures for the money and reserve money supply in 1974 in_____?

    b. In which source and on what page did you find this information?

5. You are taking a special topics in American history course on presidential campaigns in the twentieth century. You are doing your research paper on the 1976 election and must rely on newspaper accounts as sources of information. For a guide to the dates of newspapers which contain reports of events you consider important, you first turn to the 1977 edition of a source which reviews the major events of 1975-76 in the United States. From it you compile a list of campaign events with the dates you need for your newspaper research. One of the dates on your list is_____.

   a. What happened on that date which is important to your information?

   b. In which source and on what page did you find this information?

6. You are taking a seminar on political trends in Europe since World War II. There is going to be a parliamentary election in England in six weeks and the instructor has assigned each student a number of constituencies to follow by reading British newspapers available in your college library. To begin the project, you use the 1977 edition of a source discussed in this chapter to identify the current members of Parliament from the constituencies assigned to you. One of your constituencies is_____ _____.

   a. What is the name of the current representative in Commons and his or her party?

   b. In which source and on what page did you find this information?

Chapter 4

ATLASES

Objective 1: After reading this chapter, the student will
describe a situation in which an historical atlas
would be useful.
Objective 2: Given a subject, the student will provide specified
information using an historical atlas.

An atlas is a bound collection of maps. The type of maps
contained and the amount of narrative information included
varies depending on the type and purpose of the atlas. There
are basically three types:

--general reference atlases, containing physical and

political maps of the world at a given time (the focus

is current; both recent and older general atlases can be

useful to historians);

--regional or national atlases, focusing on the physical

characteristics and political boundaries of a specific

geographic area, whether a continent, a country, or

region within a country (again the focus is current and

both recent and older regional atlases are useful);

and

--thematic or subject atlases, concentrating on specific

topics, e.g., economics, demography, etc.

Atlases are versatile aids for understanding the history

of countries or continents. Often physical features (mountains,

rivers, etc.), natural resources (soil types, minerals,

vegetation), and climatic conditions (rainfall, temperature variations, etc.) are important factors influencing the history of countries and relations between nations. Maps which visually present this information aid in understanding these factors.

Although all types of atlases (see Appendix for examples of each) can be valuable tools for classroom or independent study, the focus of this chapter is on thematic atlases, specifically historical atlases. Historical atlases may depict the evolution of conditions, either worldwide or in a specific region, over an extended time period, or may deal with a specific event, such as the Civil War.

Examples of historical atlases which are useful to history students are:

Adams, James Truslow, ed. Atlas of American History. New York: Scribner's, 1943.

Over 140 black and white maps cover topics in American history from the age of exploration to the eve of the First World War. The emphasis is on political history. There is no table of contents, so the user must page through the book to discover the subject focus of the different maps. Individual place names can be located easily through the detailed index.

Lord, Clifford and Elizabeth H. Historical Atlas of the United States. Rev. ed. New York: Holt, 1953. Reprinted by Johnson Reprint Corp., 1969.

Some 300 maps depict the development of the United States from the colonial period to 1950. Population, education, transportation, military campaigns, and natural resources are some of the subjects treated. There is a detailed table of contents and a subject index.

Shepherd, William. <u>Historical Atlas</u>. 9th ed. New York: Barnes and Noble, 1964. Reprinted with revisions, 1967.

This standard atlas covers primarily the Western world. Maps are arranged chronologically. The emphasis is on political history. Both a table of contents and an index are included.

Chapter 4

ATLASES

Assignment

1. Describe a situation in which an historical atlas would be
    useful.

2. In your United States history survey course, the instructor
    has given a take-home exam which includes a map question.
    Each student has been given a list of famous battles and
    must mark the location of each on the map provided. One
    of the battles you must locate is the_____
    _____.

    a. In a source discussed in this chapter, what is the
        number and title of the plate (map) which identifies
        this battle site?

    b. In which atlas did you find this information?

3. In your course on the economic development of the United
    States, you are studying agricultural production. To
    improve your understanding of the graphs and tables in
    your text, you consult a source which provides visual
    comparisons of the volume of production of different crops
    in various regions at certain times. One of the visual
    presentations you are able to locate concerns the
    production of_____
    _____.

    a. What is the title of the atlas which contains a map
        depicting this information?

    b. What is the map number and page number of this map?

4. In one of the readings for your course on the ancient
    world, the author frequently uses place names in describing
    events, but there is no map in the book. To be sure that
    you understand the author's discussion of certain events
    you locate and use a map of_____
    _____.

    a. What is the title of an atlas which contains a map
        appropriate to your needs?

    b. What is the page number and scale of the map?

Chapter 5

SUBJECT DICTIONARIES AND ENCYCLOPEDIAS

Objective 1: After reading this chapter, the student will
describe a situation in which a subject dictionary
or subject encyclopedia would be useful in
historical research or study.

Objective 2: Given a research topic in American history, the
student will identify a relevant summary article
in a subject encyclopedia and will provide
specified information about the article.

Objective 3: Given a research topic in European economic
history, the student will identify a relevant
summary article in a subject encyclopedia and will
provide specified information about the article.

Objective 4: Given a research topic in European history, the
student will identify a relevant summary article
in a subject encyclopedia and will provide
specified information about the article.

The primary purpose of a dictionary is to indicate the

meanings of words. The words included and the extent to which

the definitions are exhaustive depend upon the type of

dictionary. There are basically four types: dictionaries of a

general nature (abridged and unabridged); those which focus on

specific aspects of language (for example, synonyms, slang,

etymology); those which translate words from one language to

another; and those which concentrate on individual subject

areas. The focus of this discussion is on the fourth type,

subject dictionaries.

Almost every academic discipline can be said to have its

own specialized "language." The function of a subject

dictionary is to briefly explain the words--whether terms or

names--which make up a particular subject's specialized jargon.

Subject dictionaries list terms unfamiliar in common usage, as well as rather ordinary terms which, within the context of a subject discipline, have taken on highly specialized and technical meanings.

History students may make use of a variety of subject dictionaries since history is a comprehensive field encompassing politics, art, religion, military tactics, and the like. For example, when studying American political history, a student might consult a political science dictionary such as the American Political Dictionary (see Appendix for a complete citation) for basic information about an unfamiliar court case, legal procedure, or government agency. As another example, students reading military history might use the Dictionary of Weapons and Military Terms (see the Appendix for a complete citation) for descriptions of weapons and how they were used during a specific time period. Students can identify available subject dictionaries by consulting a guide such as Sheehy's Guide to Reference Books (see Chapter One).

While dictionaries contain brief definitions of terms, encyclopedias contain summary essays about individual topics. There are two types: general encyclopedias which are wide-ranging in topical coverage, and subject encyclopedias which focus on topics within an individual subject discipline or group of related disciplines.

The essays in subject encyclopedias are written by recognized scholars. They are accompanied by selective bibliographies and by cross-reference listings of other essays

in the encyclopedia which may contain useful additional information. Students can therefore profitably use an essay in a
subject encyclopedia in several ways: as an initial introduction
to a topic about which they know very little; as a means of
rounding out and placing in a wider context reading they are
doing about an individual matter that falls within a wider
topic; or as the starting point for research they intend to do
on an aspect of a topic. The student engaged in research may
find an essay on the topic useful in clarifying and defining
the research project, and the bibliography accompanying the
essay may provide valuable leads for further reading.

An example of a subject encyclopedia useful to history
students is:

Adams, James T., ed. Dictionary of American History.
Rev. ed. New York: Scribner's, 1976.

    Dealing with over 7,200 subjects, this is the most
comprehensive and up-to-date subject encyclopedia on
American history. All aspects of American history from
1640 to the present, except biography, are covered. The
signed articles are arranged in alphabetical order. Due
to editorial policy, a number of articles are brief, 50 to
5,000 words, and in this regard the Dictionary differs
from most other subject encyclopedias whose essays are
generally much longer. Major topics are broken down into
component parts which are treated as separate entries,
with a generous use of cross references to tie individual
articles together. In most cases, there is a short
bibliography at the end of each article. There is a
detailed subject index.

In a type of subject encyclopedia unique to the discipline
of history, the encyclopedic set, the alphabetical arrangement
of topics characteristic of most encyclopedias is replaced by
an overall chronological arrangement. The long articles in

these multivolume sets resemble chapters treating specific topics within the overall subject focus of the set. Examples of encyclopedic sets include:

Cambridge Economic History of Europe. Cambridge, England: University Press, 1941-1966.

Treats European economic history from the Middle Ages to the mid-twentieth century. Each volume consists of separately written topical chapters. At the end of each volume there is a bibliography of major writings on each topic. Although each volume has its own index, there is no index for the entire set.

New Cambridge Modern History. Cambridge, England: University Press, 1957-1970.

This work is a revision of the Cambridge Modern History (1902-1912). It covers the period from the Renaissance to 1945. The volumes are arranged chronologically; the chapters within each volume are topical. All bibliographic material is contained in a separate volume, Roach's A Bibliography of Modern History (see Appendix for complete citation). Each volume has a detailed table of contents and index; there is no general index for all volumes. Two other encyclopedic sets, Cambridge Ancient History and Cambridge Medieval History, are standard reference works for the periods they cover.

Chapter 5

SUBJECT DICTIONARIES AND ENCYCLOPEDIAS

Assignment

1. Describe a situation in which a subject dictionary or
    subject encyclopedia would be useful in historical research
    or study.

2. In your United States history text, there is a brief dis-
    cussion of_____
    _____.
    The topic interests you and you decide to see if you can
    find enough material for a paper.

    a. Which source discussed in this chapter contains an
        article on the subject? In what volume and on what
        page(s) does the article appear?

    b. What is the title of the first item in the
        bibliography?

3. For your European economic history course, you must write
    a research paper on some aspect of_____
    _____.
    You decide to write about_____
    _____
    _____.
    To begin your research, you want to locate a summary
    treatment and bibliography on the topic.

    a. What is the name of the author of a summary article
        on the topic in a subject encyclopedia discussed in
        this chapter?

b. What is the title of the encyclopedia and the pages in the separate bibliography section where publications dealing with the topic are listed?

4. In your European history survey course, each student has the option of doing a term paper for additional credit. From the readings in your text you have taken an interest in the period_____.
You are considering doing your paper on some aspect of

_____.

In your efforts to define a precise topic, you consult an encyclopedia for an essay that deals with the overall subject.

a. What is the name of the author of an essay on the subject?

b. What is the title of the first subdivision of the essay identified in the table of contents?

c. What is the title of the encyclopedic set and the volume in which you found the essay? (List the number, not the title of the individual volume.)

Chapter 6

BIOGRAPHICAL DICTIONARIES

Objective 1:   After reading this chapter, the student will
               describe a situation in which history majors
               would use a biographical dictionary.
Objective 2:   Given the name of an individual, the student will
               use a universal biographical dictionary to find
               specified information.
Objective 3:   Given the name of an individual, the student will
               use a national biographical dictionary listed in
               this chapter to locate specified information.
Objective 4:   The student will use an occupational biographical
               dictionary to find specified information about an
               historian.

In historical reading and research, students often encounter

references to individuals about whom they may need to know more

in order to enhance their understanding of the material.

Usually a brief factual summary, rather than a detailed book-

length publication about the person, is all that is required.

Biographical dictionaries provide this sort of information,

whether the individual is living or dead, whether a fifteenth--

or twentieth--century figure.

There are several categories of biographical dictionaries.

The most comprehensive is the universal biographical dictionary

which treats people from all time periods, countries, and

occupations. When students encounter a totally unfamiliar

name, they can begin their search for information by consulting

a universal biographical dictionary. One example is:

<u>Webster's Biographical Dictionary</u>. Springfield, Mass.:
G. & C. Merriam Co., 1967.

This single volume work contains brief biographical
sketches, including dates, occupation, and historical
significance, for over 40,000 individuals. Coverage is
not restricted by period or place, although there is an
American and British bias. In addition to the individual
biographical entries, there are tables listing officials
such as presidents, British prime ministers, and sovereigns
of major countries of the world.

National or regional biographical dictionaries, a second

category, are limited in coverage to a particular geographical

area and include people from all professions and occupations

within that area. Because of the regional focus, information

is provided about many individuals who would not be listed in

the more selective universal dictionaries. Generally, coverage

in national biographical dictionaries is limited either to

prominent living persons or to famous deceased individuals, but

rarely includes both. Among the national biographical diction-

aries of living individuals are <u>Who's Who in America</u> for the

United States and <u>Who's Who</u> for Great Britain (see Appendix for

complete citations). Examples of national biographical diction-

aries of deceased individuals are:

<u>Dictionary of American Biography</u>   New York: Scribner's,
1928-37. 20 v. and Index. Supplements 1-4. New York:
Scribner's, 1944-1974.

This twenty-volume set contains biographical sketches
of over 13,000 prominent Americans deceased before 1928.
An additional two thousand individuals deceased after 1928
are covered in four supplements. For each person, dates,
occupation, family, and important accomplishments are
listed. In addition, a bibliography is appended to each
sketch. There is an index volume to the basic set. A
cumulative index to all the supplements is included in
each new supplement.

<u>Dictionary of National Biography</u>. London: Elder, 1908-09. 22 v. 2nd-7th supplements. Oxford: University Press, 1912-71. 6 v.

This is an important source for concise information on noteworthy deceased inhabitants of Great Britain and the British Empire. The basic set includes information on individuals deceased prior to 1900; the supplements bring the coverage up to 1960. Appended to each biography is a bibliography of sources to consult for further information. There is an index at the end of each volume in the basic set. The index at the end of each supplement is cumulative for all the supplements.

There are national biographical dictionaries for almost every country. Some are listed in the Appendix; a comprehensive list is included in Robert Slocum's <u>Biographical Dictionaries and Related Works</u> (see Appendix for complete citation).

In a third category of biographical dictionaries, the focus is on individuals within professional groups. These occupational biographical dictionaries include information about many people not listed in the national or universal sources. For history students, occupational biographical dictionaries can be useful in two ways. First, publications such as the <u>Biographical Directory of the U.S. Executive Branch, 1774-1971</u> and the <u>Biographical Directory of the American Congress, 1774-1971</u> (see Appendix for complete citations) are useful sources of brief, factual information about individuals who have played a role in American history. Second, when evaluating the quality of a particular historical book or article, students may want information about the author's professional contributions and qualifications. A useful source for this second type of information is:

Directory of American Scholars. 6th ed. New York:
R. R. Bowker Co., 1974.

Volume one of this four-volume set provides biographical information about more than 10,000 historians. The
data on each include dates, education, professional
experience, honors, chief fields of research interest,
major publications, and mailing address. At the end of
the volume, individuals are listed by geographical location
(state and city).

Whenever students want more than brief, summary biographical

information about an individual, they may turn to sources which

identify autobiographical and biographical books and articles.

In addition to some of the dictionaries discussed in this

chapter, several guides, such as the Harvard Guide to American

History discussed in Chapter One, perform this function.

Another source, Biography Index (see Appendix, section for

Chapter Seven, for a complete citation), has as its sole

purpose the identification of biographical books and articles.

Chapter 6

BIOGRAPHICAL DICTIONARIES

Assignment

1. Describe a situation in which a history student would use a biographical dictionary.

2. In your western civilization course, your instructor has given each student a list of names and asked for brief identifications. The first name on your list is _____ _____.

    a. What is the country of origin and what are the birth and death dates for the person?

    b. What is the title and page of a universal biographical dictionary which contains information on this person?

3. In reading you are doing for your English history course, you come across the name_____ _____. To understand the author's point, you think you need more information on the individual than the author provides. You consult a national biographical dictionary.

    a. What was the person's occupation?

    b. What is the title, volume, and page of a national biographical dictionary which contains information on this person?

4. During a lecture in your American history survey course, your instructor mentions_____ _____. After checking your text and finding no reference to this

person, you consult a national biographical dictionary.
A bibliography is appended to the sketch.

a. What is the first title listed in the bibliography?

b. What is the title, volume, and page of the national
biographical dictionary which contains information
on this person?

5. As an introduction for your class report on a book by

_____,
you want information about the author's other publications
and professional record. You consult an occupational
biographical dictionary.

a. Where did the author earn his or her Ph.D.?

b. What is the title of the dictionary and page where
you found this information?

Chapter 7

INDEXES AND ABSTRACTS

Objective 1: After reading this chapter, the student will
              distinguish between indexes and abstracts and
              will describe a situation in which either one
              would be useful.
Objective 2: Given a topic and date, the student will identify
              a relevant article listed in an index.
Objective 3: Given a topic and date, the student will identify
              a relevant article listed in an abstract.

Indexes and abstracts are used by researchers primarily to
identify journal articles on specific topics. Most indexes and
abstracts are published several times a year, with annual
cumulations. The Readers' Guide to Periodical Literature (see
Appendix for complete citation), which lists articles in
general magazines, is an index familiar to most students. More
specialized indexes and abstracts list articles published in
scholarly journals. These finding aids are important because
the articles in historical journals often update information
found in books, and in some cases constitute the only published
treatments of certain topics.

The standard citation for articles in indexes includes the
author's name, the article title, the name of the journal, the
volume and number, the date of the issue of the journal in
which the article appears, and the page numbers. Among the
indexes useful to history students are:

Humanities Index. New York: H.W. Wilson Co., v. 1-.
1974/75-.

In 1974 the Social Sciences and Humanities Index
split into two publications, one of which is the Humanities
Index. This quarterly arranges by subject articles in
some 260 journals for the fields of archaeology, classics,
area studies, folklore, history, language and literature,
literary and political criticism, the performing arts,
religion and theology, etc. A separate section at the end
of each issue indexes book reviews. There is a list of
periodical abbreviations at the beginning of each issue.

In abstracts, the citation for each article is followed by
a brief summary of its contents. This summary, or "abstract,"
often enables researchers to determine whether or not an
article is useful for their purposes, without having to locate
and read it. This can be especially important when researchers
are working in a library with a small periodical collection and
must depend on interlibrary loans to acquire a significant
number of articles. Among the abstracts which are of primary
use to the history student are:

Historical Abstracts. Santa Barbara, Calif.: American
Bibliographical Center--Clio Press, v. 1-. 1955-.

This work cites and abstracts articles relating to
the study of history from approximately 2,000 periodicals.
The volumes published from 1955 through 1970 cover the
period 1775 to 1945; those published in 1971 and 1972
cover 1775 to the present; and those published since 1973
cover 1450 to the present. Since 1971, Historical Abstracts
has been published in two parts, one covering the period
to 1914 and the other covering the years since then.
There are annual indexes, with three five-year cumulative
indexes published thus far.

America: History and Life. Santa Barbara, Calif.:
American Bibliographical Center--Clio Press, v. 1-.
1964/65-.

This abstract lists articles, book reviews, and dissertations on Canada and the United States. The articles are taken from approximately 1900 periodicals. The work is divided into four parts. Part A, "Article Abstracts and Citations," is published three times a year. Each issue lists articles, with brief annotations, by broad subject categories, and indexes these articles more specifically in the subject index. Part B, "Index to Book Reviews," is issued twice yearly. Books are listed by author. Part C, "American History Bibliography," is published annually and is a listing of articles cited in Part A, books cited in Part B, and dissertations. Part D, "Annual Index," provides cumulative subject and author indexes for Parts A, B, and C.

Chapter 7

INDEXES AND ABSTRACTS

Assignment

1. What is one difference between indexes and abstracts?

2. Describe a situation in which a student would use an index or abstract for historical research or study.

3. In your seminar on_____ the instructor has asked each student to compile a list of recent articles on an assigned topic. Your assigned topic is_____. You began your search for titles with the most recent issue of Humanities Index and have progressed to volume 1 (1974-75).

    a. What is the complete citation (author, title, journal, volume, date, and pages) for the first article listed on your topic? (Do not abbreviate the title of the journal.)

    b. On which page of the Humanities Index did you find this information?

4. In your American history senior seminar, the instructor
    has asked each student to prepare a report on some aspect
    of the history of one of the states. One of the subject
    areas which you are considering is_____
    _____.
    You began be searching in the most recent edition of an
    abstract discussed in this chapter and have progressed
    to the 1976 edition.

    a. What is the complete citation for the first article
        listed on your subject?

    b. In which abstract and on what page did you find this
        information?

5. In your seminar on Africa in the twentieth century,
    students have been asked to compile a selective reading
    list on special topics. Your topic is_____
    _____.
    You began your search for periodical articles with the
    latest issue of Historical Abstracts: Part B and are now
    using the cumulative index for _____.

    a. What is the complete citation for the first article
        on your topic?

    b. On what page did you find this information?

Chapter 8

BIBLIOGRAPHIES

Objective 1:   After reading this chapter, the student will
               describe a situation in which bibliographies are
               useful for historical study or research.
Objective 2:   Given a subject, the student will use a source
               discussed in this chapter to identify an appro-
               priate bibliography which is appended to a book
               or article.
Objective 3:   Given a subject, the student will use a source
               discussed in this chapter to identify an appro-
               priate retrospective bibliography.
Objective 4:   Given a subject, the student will use the Library
               of Congress Subject Catalog to identify a book on
               that subject.

To utilize study and research time effectively, students

must rely on sources which identify existing print materials

relevant to their topics. Bibliographies constitute a partic-

ularly important category of finding aids. An individual

bibliography might list any or all of the following: books,

periodicals, periodical articles, published documents, unpub-

lished documents, unpublished manuscripts. The focus of the

discussion in this chapter is on bibliographies as finding aids

primarily for books other than reference books and, secondarily,

for articles. Whenever students use a bibliography that does

not list journal articles as well as book titles, they should

also consult a periodical index or abstract (see Chapter Nine)

in order to compile a thorough reading list on a topic.

Some bibliographies provide only citations for the books

and articles they list; others also provide annotations. The standard bibliographic citation for books includes author, title, publisher, and place and date of publication. The standard citation for articles includes author, title, journal name, volume and number, date of publication, and page number. In most cases, the information is sufficiently complete to enable the researcher to locate the item. Annotated bibliographies provide the additional service of affording students a basis for deciding whether an individual title might be useful. An annotation consists of a brief summary of the article or book's content and a comment on its quality.

Whether annotated or not, bibliographies can appear in any one of several formats. Some are relatively short and are appended to articles or books; their purpose is to identify titles either cited in, or otherwise relevant to the topic of, the article or book. A bibliography appended to a reliable book or article can be profitably used as a guide to other readings on the topic. To identify appended bibliographies on a particular topic, students may consult:

Bibliographic Index. New York: H.W. Wilson Co., 1937-.

Bibliographic Index is issued in April and August, and in a cumulated annual volume in December. It lists, by subject, bibliographies with 50 or more entries which are published separately or as parts of books or articles in English and west European languages. Entries specify whether or not the bibliographies are annotated. Each issue begins with (1) a prefatory note which briefly explains the forms used in entries, and (2) lists of periodical abbreviations and other abbreviations used in the entries. Students should begin their search for appropriate titles with the most recent issues.

Book-length bibliographies can appear in one of two formats. Some are published periodically, for example every year, and are called current bibliographies. Others are published only once and are called retrospective bibliographies. There are retrospective bibliographies in history for important events such as the American Civil War, for distinct time periods such as the Elizabethan Age in England, and for the entire histories of regions or countries. As an example of this last type, the greater part of the Harvard Guide to American History (annotated in Chapter One) is a retrospective bibliography on American history. To identify retrospective bibliographies published since 1963, students should consult recent issues of Bibliographic Index. Those published earlier are listed in:

> Besterman, Theodore A. A World Bibliography of Bibliographies and of Bibliographical Catalogs, Calendars, Abstracts, Digests, Indexes and the Like. 4th ed. Lausanne: Societas Bibliographica, 1965-66.
>
> Approximately 117,000 bibliographies published separately prior to 1963 are listed by subject. Information provided includes the number of titles listed in the cited work. The subsections for large topics, individual countries, for example, are conveniently listed at the beginning of the overall section on the topic. There is an index of authors, editors, and titles.

Retrospective and appended bibliographies share an obvious drawback: they leave the student uninformed about titles published after their own publication date. The distinctive feature of a current bibliography is that it is periodically updated, with each edition listing titles that have appeared

since the previous edition. Generally, current bibliographies
attempt coverage of an entire subject discipline, or of a
subdivision of a discipline which has a literature of considerable proportion. There is no entirely satisfactory current
bibliography for either world history or American history. In
the annual International Bibliography of Historical Sciences,
which focuses on world history during all time periods, subject
headings and other editorial material appear in English only
every fifth year. Although Foreign Affairs Bibliography is
well-prepared and useful, offering selective annotated lists of
titles on every country, its coverage is limited to twentieth
century history and it is issued only every ten years. The
current bibliography in American history is Writings on American
History (see Appendix for complete citations of the titles in
this paragraph), which, for the period 1902-1961 lists books
and articles, but after 1961 lists only articles.

A bibliography which is nearly universal in its subject
focus may be used as a substitute when more specialized bibliographies are not available. It should be used as a supplement
when it is more up-to-date than available specialized bibliographies. A prestigious national library, such as the British
Library or the Library of Congress, houses copies of most of
the important books on all topics, and in many languages, that
are available in the country. Therefore, the subject catalog
of the Library of Congress, available in most college and
university libraries, can be used as a reasonably comprehensive
current bibliography on most topics.

U.S. Library of Congress. <u>Subject Catalog; A</u>
<u>Cumulative List of Works Represented by Library</u>
<u>of Congress Printed Cards</u>. Washington: 1950-.

    Published in quarterly, yearly, and five year cumu-
lative editions since 1950, the <u>Subject Catalog</u> lists
books catalogued by the Library of Congress and other
major libraries in the United States. It is the most
comprehensive single bibliography listing works on every
subject and from all parts of the world which have become
available during the period it covers. Subject headings
are cross-referenced.

Chapter 8

BIBLIOGRAPHIES

Assignment

1. Describe a situation in which bibliographies are useful
    for historical research.

2. In your course on United States diplomatic history, you
    are compiling a reading list for a term paper on some
    aspect of United States foreign relations with _____
    _____.
    You have consulted a retrospective bibliography of
    American history. You now want to identify any books and
    articles that may have been published after that retro-
    spective bibliography was compiled. You therefore con-
    sult a source that lists bibliographies appended to
    recent books and articles. You began with the most
    recent editions of that source and have progressed to
    the _____cumulative edition.

    a. What is the author and title of the first book
        listed in that source which has an appended
        bibliography relevant to your topic?

    b. In which source and on what page did you find
        this information?

3. You are taking a directed reading course on_____
    _____.
    One requirement set by your instructor is that one-half
    of your reading must be on a special topic, and you are
    considering _____
    _____.
    You check a source discussed in this chapter which lists
    retrospective bibliographies published prior to 1963, for
    titles of English language retrospective bibliographies
    covering the topic.

    a. What is the author and title of the first English
        language retrospective bibliography listed for
        that topic?

      b.   In which source and in what volume and column did
          you find this information?

4.   For your senior thesis, you have decided to write a paper
      on some aspect of the _____

      _____
      and want to compile a list of available books. You have
      consulted specialized sources and are now using a current
      general bibliography which lists most titles available in
      the United States. You began your search with the most
      recent edition and have now reached the_____
      cumulative edition.

      a.   What is the complete citation for the first English
          language title listed for your topic?

      b.   In what source, and in what volume, and on what page
          did you find this information?

Chapter 9

SCHOLARLY JOURNALS

Objective 1:   After reading this chapter, the student will
               describe a situation in which an historical
               journal would be useful.

Objective 2:   Given a specific issue of an historical journal,
               the student will answer specific questions about
               its content and format.

Objective 3:   The student will use a source discussed in this
               chapter to identify an historical journal
               dealing with a specific region.

Given a topic for study or research, students generally
turn first, and most often solely, to book-length treatments of
that topic. The purpose of this chapter is to suggest the
considerable utility of scholarly journals. Through the
articles and book reviews they contain, scholarly journals
serve important functions which make them an especially valuable
source of information for students, particularly as they
undertake independent study or research.

The articles in scholarly journals, written by specialists
and critically evaluated by other scholars prior to being
accepted for publication, often represent the most recent
additions to an academic discipline's shared store of knowledge,
or to its debate, on a particular topic. An article may deal
with a topic that has not yet been treated and may never be
treated in a book-length publication; or it may contain new
information about, or a new interpretation of, a subject
already covered in book-length publications. In either case,

students interested in compiling a well-rounded and up-to-date reading list on a topic can often only insure those qualities if they seek out articles on the topic in scholarly journals.

The book reviews in scholarly journals are of equal utility. Suppose, by way of example, that a student wants to undertake reading, either for independent study or for a research paper, on resistance movements in countries occupied by the Germans during the Second World War. There are a number of book-length studies of those movements. In the quality of research and presentation, some may be very good, some mediocre, and some unreliable. Some of the very good studies may have a special focus--on resistance newspapers, for example--that makes them inappropriate to the student's needs. A book review in a scholarly journal, by summarizing content and evaluating quality, provides a basis for a decision about a book's utility. When faced with a choice among several books, students will save time, and will make selections that are as informed as possible, if they consult book reviews.

Historians publish a large number of journals, some rather general in scope, and some devoted to a particular region, time period, or subfield of the discipline, such as social history. Two examples of scholarly journals with which undergraduate history majors should be familiar are:

American Historical Review. Washington, D.C.: American Historical Association, 1895-. Reprint: Kraus.

The official journal of the American Historical Association, this publication is generally regarded as

the most prestigious historical journal in the United
States. The articles are not topically limited to any
country or time period. In each issue there are well over
100 reviews of books on all historical subjects, arranged
by subject. There are annual indexes of articles and book
reviews, as well as periodic cumulative indexes.

Journal of American History. (Formerly: Mississippi
Valley Historical Review.) Bloomington, Indiana:
Organization of American Historians, 1914-.

This publication of the Organization of American
Historians is the most respected journal devoted to
American history. It contains articles on all aspects of
American history and, in each issue, an extensive book
review section. There is a cumulative index for the years
1914-1964, when the journal appeared under its original
title.

Depending upon their interests, students may turn to

English language historical journals which focus either upon

particular geographic areas other than the United States as a

whole, or upon individual subfields of history. There are, for

example, journals which focus on regions of the United States,

and many which focus on individual states. Students of European

history may select from among journals focusing on different

time periods, regions, or countries. There are journals

devoted to the historical study of Africa, Asia, and the Middle

East. There are journals which focus on economic history,

social history, intellectual history, and so on. A list

suggestive of the range of historical journals is contained in

the Appendix. For a more complete list, with descriptive

annotations, consult:

Katz, William. Magazines for Libraries. 2nd ed.
New York: R. R. Bowker, 1972.

This work contains publication information and
descriptive and evaluative annotations for over 4,500
periodicals and newspapers. Titles are organized into
approximately 100 subject areas. A 1974 supplement,
organized in basically the same way, with some subject
heading changes, brings the listings more up-to-date,
adding 1,800 titles. Its index covers both the original
volume and the supplement. In the History section of both
volumes, all journals except those with geographic focus
on the United States, Canada, and their states and provinces,
are listed under the General subheading.

While a familiarity with important historical journals is

necessary for students who wish to keep currently informed

about the progress of scholarship in their field, students

usually turn to journals with the specific purpose of locating

articles on a precise topic or finding reviews of a particular

book. Given those purposes, finding aids such as the indexes

and abstracts discussed in Chapter Seven are essential keys to

periodical literature.

Chapter 9

SCHOLARLY JOURNALS

Assignment

1. Describe a situation in which it would be appropriate to use an historical journal.

2. In your history resources and methods course, your instructor wants each student to become familiar with some of the important historical journals. She gives each student a list of specific issues of several journals, and a set of questions about each issue. One of the journals on your list is the _____. Using _____ of this journal answer the following questions.

   a. Who is the author of the article entitled _____ _____ and where does the author teach?

   b. Identify the title of the article by _____ _____.

   c. Using the notes accompanying this article _____ _____ _____.

   d. Identify the author of the book review of _____ _____. (Do not identify the author of the book.)

3. In your course on state and local history, the instructor asks you to identify the title of a journal focusing on the history of your state. You live in _____.

    a. Using a source discussed in this chapter, what is the complete title of a journal devoted to the history of your state?

    b. In which source and on what page did you find this information?

Chapter 10

EVALUATING BOOK-LENGTH STUDIES

Objective 1:   After reading this chapter, the student will
               explain the reasons for evaluating research
               sources and will describe methods for doing
               so.
Objective 2:   Given the author, title, and publication date for
               a book, the student will use the Humanities Index
               to identify a journal containing a review of the
               book.
Objective 3:   Given the author, title, and publication date for
               a book, the student will locate a review in a
               book review journal.

Book-length studies will in most cases constitute the

greater part of a student's reading list on an individual

research or independent study topic. Finding aids used to

identify book titles appropriate to a particular topic were

discussed in Chapter Seven. Much depends upon the care with

which students select from among the titles they do identify;

if the sources of information used in research and study are

unreliable, the results will necessarily be unsatisfactory.

There are two principal ways to evaluate a book-length study of

a particular topic: by relying upon book reviews, and by

examining the bibliographic quality of the book itself.

Book Review Sources

     Since 1975, reviews appearing in most of the major histor-

ical journals have been indexed in the book review section of

the Humanities Index and in America: History and Life, Part B:

Index to Book Reviews (see Chapter Seven). The reviews are

listed by the name of the author of the book; the journal, volume, date, and page of the review are provided.

There is generally a considerable time lag, often more than a year, between the publication of a book and the appearance of a review in a scholarly journal. The need for more current reviews has given rise to a new type of journal, made up entirely of scholarly book reviews. For history, there are two such review journals:

History: Reviews of New Books. Washington, D.C.: Heldref Publications, 1972-.

This publication, issued ten times each year, contains reviews of books on a wide range of historical topics. Usually a review appears within a year of the book's publication. Approximately 60 books are reviewed in each issue and the reviews run 400 to 500 words. The reviews are not as lengthy and detailed as those which appear in journals like the American Historical Review.

Reviews in American History. Westport, Conn.: Redgrave Information Resources Corp., 1973-.

The primary purpose of this journal is to publish lengthy and scholarly reviews of books in American history and related disciplines. Each issue contains approximately 25 essay-length reviews. A review usually appears within a year of the publication of the book.

Bibliographic Character of the Work

Often by examining certain features of a book closely, a student can make an informed judgment about its quality. The preface and introduction usually tell something about the author, why the work was written, and what methodology and research went into the preparation of the work. If the author is an acknowledged authority in the field, this is often mentioned. If there is little or no information about the author, students may consult a biographical source such as the Directory of American Scholars (see Chapter Six) for a summary of his or her scholarly achievements.

The footnotes and the bibliography are usually indicative of the reliability of the book. If few or no original documents have been used, or if major works in the field have not been cited or evaluated, the student has reason to question the quality of the work.

Finally, the reputation of the publisher or organization which sponsors a particular book can provide the student with a clue to the reliability of the information it contains. Some publishers have more rigid standards of scholarship than others. For example, the requirements of university presses are generally very high; major university presses, such as Oxford, Cambridge, Princeton, and Harvard, can be counted on as discriminating publishers of historical studies.

Chapter 10

EVALUATING BOOK-LENGTH STUDIES

Assignment

1. Explain the reasons for evaluating research sources and describe one method of doing so.

2. One of the sources you are considering for a research paper is_____
_____by_____.
You would like to know how other historians have evaluated the book. To locate a review, you turn to the book review section of the Humanities Index (annotated in Chapter Seven). Since the book was published in 1974, you began with the 1974/75 volume and have progressed to the 1975/76 volume.

   a. What is the complete citation (journal, volume, pages, date, and reviewer) of the first book review listed? (Do not abbreviate the name of the journal.)

   b. On what page did you find the review?

3. For your independent study course, you are preparing a list of recently published books on an assigned topic. You have identified a number of books and must be selective about those you actually read so you decide to read scholarly reviews of each book. One of your books is
_____
by_____.
Since it has been published recently, you turn to current issues of History: Reviews of New Books, and you find a review in_____.

   a. Who is the author of the review? (Not the author of the book.)

b. Where does the author of the review teach?

c. On what page(s) did you find the review?

4. In your American history seminar, the instructor has given
   each student a list of recently published books and asked
   for short summaries of scholarly book reviews. One of
   your books is_____

   _____
   by_____.
   Since it has been published recently, you turn to current
   issues of <u>Reviews in American History</u>, and you find a
   review in_____.

   a. Who is the author of the review? (Not the author of
      the book.)

   b. Where does the author of the review teach?

   c. On what page(s) did you find the review?

Chapter 11

NEWSPAPERS

Objective 1: After reading this chapter, the student will
describe the principal uses of newspapers for
research in history.
Objective 2: Using the Ayer Directory of Publications, the
student will identify, and provide specified
publication information for, a newspaper published
in a specific city.
Objective 3: Given a topic and a time period, the student will
use an index to identify the date, page, column,
and summary information for a relevant article in
the New York Times.
Objective 4: Given a topic and a time period, the student will
use an index to identify the date, page, column,
and summary information for a relevant article in
the Times (London).

The discussions in this and the next chapter will be of

two different types of source materials available to historians

and history majors when they undertake original research. The

term "original research" implies work done primarily with

materials other than studies of a topic, whether books or

articles, written by scholars. The materials used by historians

include sources such as the private papers of statesmen,

unpublished official documents housed in archives, and personal

reminiscences, either written or, increasingly in recent years,

in the form of taped interviews. The combination of materials

used by an individual historian depends upon the subject matter

under study and the availability of sources. The ways in which

the various sources are used depend upon the scholar's skill

and judgment. The choice of source materials for discussion in this and the next chapter is not based on judgments about their merits relative to other types of source materials. Rather, it is based on a pragmatic consideration: newspapers and government publications are generally far more easily available to students, either at their own institutions or through interlibrary loan, than are other types of source material.

Exercising scholarly judgment about their reliability, historians use newspaper stories as eyewitness accounts of events. This particular example of the uses scholars make of newspapers can be illustrated with reference to research on local, state, and national history.

For research on local history, newspapers are often an especially important source. In many cases, researchers first find mention of a particular event in a newspaper account. Using facts contained in the story as clues about where to look next, they may then seek out additional sources of information about the event. In some instances, they find that newspaper accounts constitute the only available record of a particular event.

For research on state history, newspapers can add significantly to data collected from other sources. For example, newspapers published in state capitals often contain extensive coverage of state politics. Not only the votes of a legislature and the policies of the executive branch, but also the comments, opinions, and explanations of legislators and executive officials are recorded.

For information on newspapers published in a particular locality, students may consult the current and, depending upon the time period under study, old editions of:

Ayer Directory of Publications. Philadelphia: Ayer Press, 1880-. (Formerly titled N. W. Ayer and Son's Directory of Newspapers and Periodicals.)

A directory of newspapers and periodicals published four or more times yearly in the United States, Canada, the Bahamas, Bermuda, and the Republics of Panama and the Philippines. In the main section of this work, publications are listed by location. Information includes, in the case of newspapers: date of establishment, frequency of publication, political identity (Democrat, Republican, Independent), circulation, address, editor, and publishing company.

Newspapers which give extensive and reliable coverage to news of national significance can be of use to historians in several ways. In some cases they may serve as a principal source of information. For example, so long as police records remain closed, a researcher interested in major anti-Vietnam war demonstrations will have to rely on newspaper accounts of the sizes of crowds, their actions, and the statements of speakers. As an additional example, for so long as the papers of Joseph McCarthy remain closed to scholars, newspaper accounts of his speeches and activities outside the Senate will remain an important source for research about his career. More often than as a principal source, newspapers serve as an auxiliary source in research on national issues. For example, scholars writing on American foreign policy can supplement the documents they use with newspaper quotes from government officials, which in some cases elucidate the attitudes and specific aims behind certain policies.

Among American newspapers respected for their coverage of national and international news are the New York Times, the Washington Post and the Christian Science Monitor. The special focus of some newspapers, such as the Wall Street Journal, makes them especially important sources. Subject indexes for all but the first of these newspapers are listed in the Appendix. Researchers using the New York Times should consult:

New York Times Index. New York: The New York Times, 1913-.

    Provides subject access to New York Times news stories, editorials and other features. Published every two weeks, it is cumulated annually. Each entry begins with a subject, followed by references to other sections in the index (if there are any). Then the article is summarized. For the sake of brevity, the citation identifies each month by one or two letters, followed by the date, a roman numeral for a section and an arabic page number, and sometimes a column number, prefaced by a colon. The year is always identified on the cover and title page and is essential information to copy when copying citations. One important item to note in using this index is that the cross references which directly follow the subject in each entry must be checked in the index to obtain a complete citation. The user cannot identify the exact location of the articles noted in this section without doing so.

As well as recording public events, newspapers are vehicles for the expression of opinion. The editorials and the news stories which record statements by spokesmen for various interest groups are material for the historian weighing public sentiment in the retelling of events.

For researchers studying the histories of foreign countries, the news and expressions of opinion in the papers of those countries can be important sources. For research on the political history of countries in which political parties have traditionally published their own newspapers--this is the case in France, for example--those newspapers are especially important sources for, among other things, the histories of those parties and of political debates of national issues.

For many American undergraduates, a lack of accessibility and/or a lack of language facility prohibit the use of foreign newspapers. These problems have been lessened somewhat in the last few decades by the appearance of press digests which excerpt, in English translation, selected foreign press stories and editorials. Some of these digests are listed in the Appendix. For coverage of Great Britain, its empire and later the Commonwealth, and European developments, students may make use of reputable British newspapers, in particular the Manchester Guardian and The Times. Use of The Times in research is facilitated by:

Times, London (Indexes). Times Index. Reading, England: Newspaper Archive Developments Limited, 1906-.

Currently published monthly and cumulated quarterly, this index provides subject access to The Times, The Sunday Times, The Times Literary Supplement, and The Times Higher Education Supplement. In the latest editions, each entry contains a subject followed by a brief summary of this article. The month is written out or abbreviated and is followed by the day. Columns are noted with a letter from a to g. At the top of each page the year is identified and this information is an essential component of a citation if one hopes to locate the article. Inasmuch as the official index goes back only to 1906, researchers must use Palmer's Index (cited in full in the Appendix) for the period from 1790 to 1905.

Chapter 11

NEWSPAPERS

Assignment

1. Describe the principal uses of newspapers for research in history.

2. As a student taking a course in local history at the University of Wisconsin, you have been asked to do a research paper on some aspect of the history of _____Wisconsin. Since microfilm copies of local newspapers are kept on file at the State Historical Society of Wisconsin, one of the sources available to you is the newspaper published in that locality. Using the 1977 edition of the Ayer Directory of Publications:

   a. What is the name of the newspaper published in that locality?

   b. When was it established?

   c. On what page did you find this information?

3. In your seminar course on Africa since the colonial era your instructor assigns each student a country and asks for a summary of major events during certain years. The country assigned to you is_____, and one of the years is_____. One of the reference works you use to compile a list of sources of information is the New York Times Index. On a separate card, you record the summary and citation for each news story you may want to consult.

   a. What is the summary of the first story listed under your topic?

b. What is the complete citation for this story (month, date, section [if Sunday], page, column)?

c. On what page of the index did you find this information?

4. You are taking a special topics seminar on the welfare state in Europe. Each student has been asked to do a paper on a particular program, and you have chosen Britain's National Health Service. You decide to trace the events involving the Service as reported in the press over a five-year period. One of the sources you use is the Times Index.

a. What is the summary of the first story cited in the _____volume?

b. What is the full citation for this story (month, date, page)?

c. On what page did you find this information?

Chapter 12

GOVERNMENT PUBLICATIONS

Objective 1: After reading this chapter, the student will
describe a situation in which government publications would be useful for historical research.
Objective 2: Using a source discussed in this chapter, the
student will identify the current checklist of
publications for a particular state.
Objective 3: Using a source discussed in this chapter, the
student will identify a state publication on a
specific topic.
Objective 4: Using two of the sources discussed in this chapter,
the student will identify a U. S. government
publication on a specific topic.

The term "government publications" refers to the printed

public documents of local governments, state governments, and

the federal government, as well as foreign governments (at the

local, regional, and national levels), and international

governmental organizations. These materials include, for

example, the official records of the meetings of deliberative

bodies, from town councils to national parliaments. They

include the texts of laws, of court decisions, and of the

public hearings and rulings of administrative and regulatory

agencies; and the periodic activity reports of executive and

administrative agencies. They also include, usually after a

discreet number of years, selected foreign policy documents.

As a final example, but for researchers hardly the least

important, they include the studies of economic and social

developments and problems which have been undertaken or

commissioned by official agencies at all levels, from the local to the international.

Government publications afford historians and history students materials for research on individual topics in political, military, diplomatic, economic, social, and other subfields of history. They afford material to researchers whose interests focus on topics that have to do with the whole of the American nation, or with an individual state, a particular locality, a foreign country, or a region of the world.

In considering the possible utility of government publications, it should not be assumed that only documents generated at the national level constitute proper material for research on a national problem or episode, or that only state or local publications are suitable for research on state and local history, or that only the publications of a particular country are suitable for the study of that country. The federal government annually gathers a considerable amount of information about the individual states. Conversely, historians have shed a great deal of light on the nature of a "national" episode such as the Progressive Era by carefully studying the Progressive Movement at the state and local levels. International agencies often gather a great deal of data about conditions or events in individual countries. As a final example, the foreign policy documents of one country may provide a record of rather candid comments by leaders of another country, shedding considerable light on their own domestic problems and policies.

When using government publications, students should, of course, exercise normal scholarly caution. The fact that a document is "official" is no automatic guarantee of the accuracy of statistics it might contain. That accuracy depends on the methods of the agency which compiled the statistics and on the conditions in which it operated. As an example of a different sort, what a public official says for the record will not necessarily reflect his or her real thinking or policy on a particular issue.

In sum, the use of government publications, like the use of any other source material, requires good judgment. It also requires familiarity with the methods and means for identifying and gaining access to individual publications relevant to a particular topic. Available reference materials for the identification of government publications are the subject of the remainder of this chapter.

REFERENCE AIDS

Given the vast number of government publications, there are, not surprisingly, a great number of sources which identify individual titles. Therefore, the first task for researchers is to select reference sources appropriate to their needs. The most comprehensive list and discussion of finding aids for the publications of all governments and international agencies is:

Palic, Vladimir M. Government Publications: A Guide to Bibliographic Tools. 4th ed. Washington, D. C.: Library of Congress, 1975.

Checklists, catalogues, and other sources identifying publications are listed in separate sections for: the branches, departments and agencies of the federal government; state and local governments; international organizations; and foreign governments. Both current and retrospective sources are identified and briefly annotated.

Federal Government Publications

Because the United States government distributes its publications to a network of libraries across the country (called depository libraries), federal publications are generally accessible to researchers, either directly or through inter-library loan. For the identification of late nineteenth and twentieth century federal government documents consult:

U.S. Superintendent of Documents. Monthly Catalog of United States Government Publications. Washington, D.C.: Government Printing Office, 1895-.

This is the most complete catalogue of federal documents available. The detailed indexes--subject, author/agency, and title--identify individual items by entry number. Entries identify personal author (if any), pagination, date, illustration notes, series title, and the Superintendent of Documents number. U. S. documents are arranged by this number in many libraries, especially those that are depositories.

Cumulative Subject Index to the Monthly Catalog of U. S. Government Publications, 1900-1971. Washington, D. C.: Carrollton Press, 1973.

A comprehensive subject index to the more than one million publications included in the Monthly Catalog from 1900 to 1971. Under each subject heading, individual publications are arranged alphabetically by key-word-in-title. Each title is followed by a series of numbers which indicate the location of the complete citation in the Monthly Catalog. For example, a publication followed by the number (65) 14901 would be found in the 1965 Monthly Catalog under the entry number 14901.

Other catalogues and indexes covering federal documents issued during earlier time periods are listed in the Appendix.

Students wanting a discussion of federal publications that is
far more detailed than this one or the one contained in Palic's
volume should consult Lawrence F. Schmeckebier, <u>Government
Publications and Their Use</u>. (See Appendix for complete
citation.)

State and Local Government Publications

The public documents of local governments, particularly
when used with local newspapers, can be rewarding sources for
historians. For the identification and use of these records,
however, there is usually no substitute for on-the-spot work at
a local archival agency or government office. The few aids
which do exist for identifying local documents are listed in
Palic, <u>Government Publications</u>. There is no singly comprehensive
source identifying the publications of all of the states. The
most inclusive source lists those received by the Library of
Congress, which by no means includes all state publications.

> U. S. Library of Congress. <u>Monthly Checklist of State
> Publications</u>. Washington, D. C.: Government Printing
> Office, 1910-.

> The Library of Congress annually receives well over
> 10,000 publications of the American states and territories.
> These are listed alphabetically by state, and for each
> state alphabetically by issuing agency. Publications of
> associations of state officials and regional organizations
> are included in a special section. Full bibliographic
> information is given, including content notes for
> composite reports. A cumulative subject/author index is
> issued annually.

Since not all state publications can be identified through
the <u>Monthly Checklist</u>, the individual checklists issued by most
states are useful sources for the researcher, although they are

not widely available. Checklists published by the individual
states are identified in Palic, Government Publications. It is
often the case that a special state or university library
serves as a depository for all publications of an individual
state. Once a state document has been identified, an attempt
can be made to secure the item through interlibrary loan.
Copies of recent publications can often be obtained by writing
directly to state agencies.

International Organizations and Foreign
Government Publications

Palic's Government Publications lists and annotates
sources that identify the publications of foreign governments
and international organizations. The League of Nations, the
United Nations, and the International Labor Organization are
among the international organizations for which finding aids
are relatively adequate. (These are listed in the Appendix.)
The United Nations and the Organization of American States
distribute some of their publications to depository networks
similar to, but much less extensive than, that of the federal
government. Students attending universities with major research
libraries will have direct access both to finding aids and to
many publications of several international organizations and
foreign governments. Students working at smaller libraries may
find some publications of foreign governments and international
organizations housed there and, by working with an instructor
and interlibrary loan, may gain access to others.

Chapter 12

GOVERNMENT PUBLICATIONS

Assignment

1. Describe a situation in which government publications would be useful for historical research.

2. You are a resident of_____
   attending school out-of-state. To earn independent study credit during your summer vacation you have arranged to do a paper on historic sites in your state. Before deciding whether you will write about a specific site, preservation of sites, or some other aspect of this general topic, you compile a reading list of available material. To find out if there are state publications on the topic, you consult a source discussed in this chapter. You began with the most recent annual compilation of that source and have progressed to the_____
   annual volume.

   a. What is the first item dealing with historic sites in your state?

   b. In which source and on what page did you find this information?

3. As a senior at a university in_____
   you want to do your senior thesis on some aspect of the state's history, using primary materials. You compile a list of current and retrospective sources which identify your state's publications.

   a. What is the full citation for the current source?

   b. In which source and on what page did you find this information?

4. For your seminar on World War II, you are doing a paper on

_____

_____

_____.

You have already identified books and articles pertaining
to the topic and are now checking to see if any relevant
publications have been issued by the federal government.
To check quickly the 1900-1971 period, you begin with the
Cumulative Subject Index to the Monthly Catalog.

a. What is the Monthly Catalog year and entry number for
a publication on the topic?

b. What are the title, copyright date, and number of
pages of that publication?

Chapter 13

RESEARCH PAPER MECHANICS AND METHODOLOGY

Objective 1: After reading this chapter, the student will utilize the techniques and strategies discussed to accomplish the preparatory work for a research paper, up to and including the compilation of a bibliography. Specifically, the student will:

(a) narrow a topic down;
(b) identify and use reference works such as encyclopedias for background information;
(c) identify and use appropriate indexes, abstracts, bibliographies;
(d) develop a list of appropriate subject headings to use in indexes, abstracts, the subject catalogue, etc.;
(e) utilize other resources to full advantage, for example, by exploiting bibliographies and footnotes in books and articles and the information on a catalogue card;
(f) maintain a search record;
(g) prepare bibliography cards using standard citation forms.

The topic of a research paper should be chosen carefully. The student should consider the following questions at the start, rather than after much time has been spent doing research; for if the answers to them are negative, research time already spent may prove to have been time wasted:

Can the topic be <u>investigated</u> well?

For most undergraduate papers, this reduces to the question of whether there is sufficient research material relevant to the topic available locally--either housed in the university's library or easily obtainable through interlibrary loan.

Can the project be <u>done</u> well?

There are objective and subjective factors to consider here. Among the former, perhaps the most important is the scope of the research topic. Students who take on topics that are too large will end with superficial research in available sources, and, inevitably, superficial and incomplete treatments of their topics in their papers. In addition to selecting topics that will not conflict with time requirements, it is advisable for students to select topics about which they know something initially, which will hold their interest, and which will require them to evaluate, form judgments, and come to definite conclusions. These considerations about interest and requirements may be important determinants of the amount of work students are willing to do, and the amount of satisfaction with which they will do it.

After selecting a topic, the time devoted to collecting information can be spent in the most efficient way possible if some basic library research techniques are utilized. Specifically, this chapter will focus on research mechanics (e.g., copying complete citations on bibliography cards) and research methodology (e.g., selecting appropriate reference tools).

MECHANICS

Complete Citations

Often research time is wasted back-tracking because certain mechanical tasks were not properly done initially. It is useful, for example, to copy, in correct form on separate cards, complete citations for every book, article, etc., for which a reference is found and which is or might be consulted. Among other things, this procedure will afford a complete, current record of sources which have been or will be used; eliminate retracing steps later to find necessary bibliographic information on sources which have been used; afford a record of sources which weren't available during the initial search; and allow requests for interlibrary loan to be filled out without having to return to the source of the citation for complete bibliographic information. Finally, at the end, no source will have to be rechecked for the precise title, author, publication date, and other information necessary to prepare a bibliography for the completed paper.

In citations, history students should use the standard forms for bibliography in the MLA Style Sheet (see Appendix for complete citation). The following are examples:

Books

Silver, David Mayer. Lincoln's Supreme Court. Urbana: University of Illinois Press, 1956.

Articles

Havens, Thomas R. H. "Women and War in Japan, 1937-45." American Historical Review, 80 (1975):913-34.

Government Publications

U. S. Department of State. United States Relations with China. Washington, D.C.: Government Printing Office, 1949.

Developing a Subject Headings List

During the initial stages of research, students should develop a list of the subject headings they will use when consulting the card catalogue, bibliographies, indexes and abstracts. An inclusive list of possible headings is advantageous, because not all of these reference sources use the same subject headings for indexing. Thus, the more topical categories students have listed, the more likely they are to locate useful material in all of the reference sources they consult. For example, a student writing on some aspect of the French and Indian War may find useful titles listed under:

    United States--History--French and Indian War, 1775-1763

    Quebec Campaign, 1759

    Ticonderoga, N.Y.--History--Capture, 1759

    Anglo-French War, 1755-1763

    Indians of North America--Wars--1759-1815

    Seven Years' War, 1756-1763

The Library of Congress Subject Headings (see Appendix for complete citation) is a useful source for quickly identifying a number of subject heading alternatives. This two-volume work contains a list of the headings which are used in the subject catalogues of most university libraries, as well as a list of related headings for each subject. When beginning a research project, students should note the subject headings listed in this source and then as the research proceeds, add new headings which seem appropriate.

Use of Catalogue Card Information

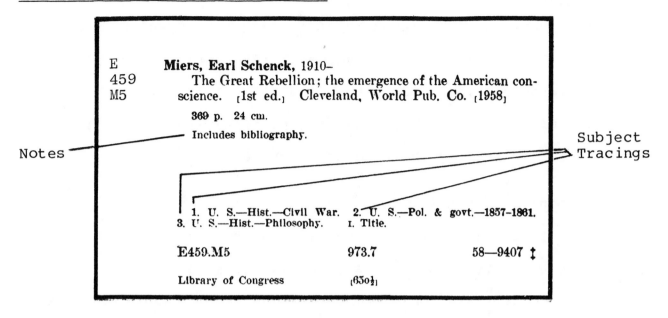

Notes

Subject
Tracings

E
459
M5

Miers, Earl Schenck, 1910–
       The Great Rebellion; the emergence of the American con-
science. ₁1st ed.₁ Cleveland, World Pub. Co. ₁1958₁
       369 p. 24 cm.
       Includes bibliography.

       1. U. S.—Hist.—Civil War. 2. U. S.—Pol. & govt.—1857–1861.
3. U. S.—Hist.—Philosophy. I. Title.

E459.M5   973.7   58—9407 ‡

Library of Congress   ₁65o½₁

In addition to the call number, cards in the library's card
catalogue provide other useful information. If a book has a
bibliography or bibliographical footnotes, a brief note in the
center of the card indicates that it does, and sometimes
indicates the pages of the book on which the bibliography will
be found. For example, the book on the card illustrated above
has a bibliography. This information should be included on the
bibliography card the student prepares for the book. Books
with bibliographies should be checked first; the bibliographies
might lead directly to useful sources, and save the student
some work with general bibliographies, abstracts and indexes,
and with some of the material listed in them which might deal
only marginally with the research topic.

       The subject tracings on catalogue cards identify all the
subject headings under which the book is listed in the subject

section of the card catalogue. For the book in the example on the previous page, cards are filed under U. S.-History-Civil War, U. S.-Politics and Government-1857-1861, and U. S.-History-Philosophy. The student who finds that the Miers book is useful for a particular research project may find additional useful sources by checking under these headings.

Keeping a Search Record

In research projects carried out over a period of time, students often redo some search work or miss valuable sources. To save time and to insure a thorough search, a research record should be kept. This can be done conveniently on three-by-five cards--one for each step in the research. An individual card should indicate one source (index, abstract, bibliography, etc.), and the subject headings and dates covered in that source. As an example:

Humanities Index

April 1974 - March 1977

Topic: War of the Huguenots

Headings Used:

St. Bartholomew's day, Massacre of (1572)

Huguenots

In addition, students should maintain a general card that lists together, in abbreviated form, all sources used. These steps will eliminate the possibility of needless duplication of effort and can help to ensure a thorough coverage of available materials.

RESEARCH METHODOLOGY

Adequate initial planning is one of the more important requirements of efficient library research. The better the methods, the greater the amount of information the student is likely to locate in the time spent in the library. On the following pages are flow charts which describe generalized research strategies for locating books and periodicals for a research paper. Not all papers will require using every step, and not all library research is best accomplished by using these strategies. These strategies can serve as suggestive examples for student researchers.

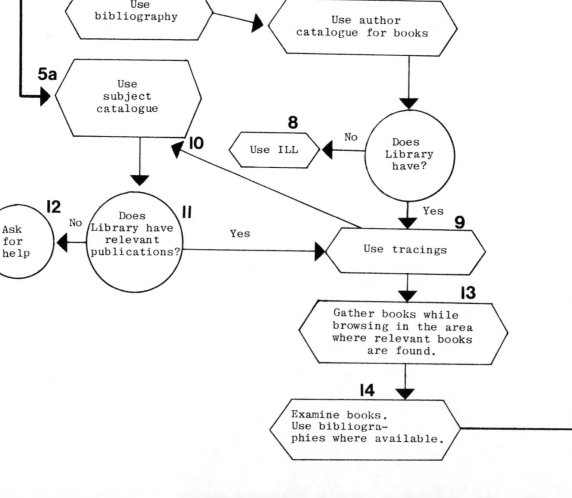

START SEARCH

1 Know general reference source?

No → **2** IDENTIFY useful reference

Yes **3** Use reference source

5 Identify available bibliography

No ← **4** Bibliography?

6 Use bibliography

7 Use author catalogue for books

5a Use subject catalogue

8 Use ILL ← No — Does Library have?

10

12 Ask for help ← No — **11** Does Library have relevant publications? — Yes → **9** Use tracings

Yes **9** Use tracings

13 Gather books while browsing in the area where relevant books are found.

14 Examine books. Use bibliographies where available.

Book Flow Chart Directions

1. When beginning research, identify a general source which supplies background information. Subject encyclopedias (Chapter Five) and textbooks are examples of publications useful at the start of a project.

2. If you do not know a general source, attempt to identify one by consulting a guide (see Chapter One). Also, your instructor or a librarian may be able to help you identify a general source.

3. With the aid of the general source, attempt to define your topic as precisely as possible, and

4. Prepare bibliography cards on relevant books and articles in the bibliography, if there is one in the general source.

5. If there is no bibliography in the general source, locate one by using a guide (see Chapter One), or one of the sources discussed in Chapter Eight which identifies bibliographies, or consult with your instructor or a librarian, or

5a. Consult your library's subject catalogue. If your library owns a specialized bibliography on your topic, it will be listed under the subject, in the subdivision for bibliography, e.g., Indians of North America - Bibliography.

6. Having located a bibliography (for a discussion see Chapter Eight), select materials which seem appropriate and make bibliography cards.

7. Check the author or title catalogue to determine whether your library owns the materials you identified through your previous efforts (for periodical articles you have listed, see step seven in the next flow chart).

8. If the library does not own some of the materials you need, request the materials through interlibrary loan (ask a librarian about procedures).

9. Use the card catalogue to determine which of the books you selected have bibliographies. Also, check the subject tracings and add new subject headings to your master list.

10-11. Using your master list of subject headings, consult your library's subject catalogue to determine whether the library has books relevant to your topic published since the bibliography you used; and for relevant books, copy complete citations, list pertinent notes and look for any new subject tracings that would be useful.

12. If at this point you feel your bibliography is inadequate, see a librarian or your instructor to evaluate your research.

13. Once you have identified relevant items owned by the library, go to the shelves, and, while gathering your books, examine others for which you have no citations but whose titles indicate they might deal with your topic.

14. Check the bibliographies in the books you have selected. If you do not have citations for some of the items you find, you may want to make additional bibliography cards and attempt to locate these materials later.

WB 88

Periodicals

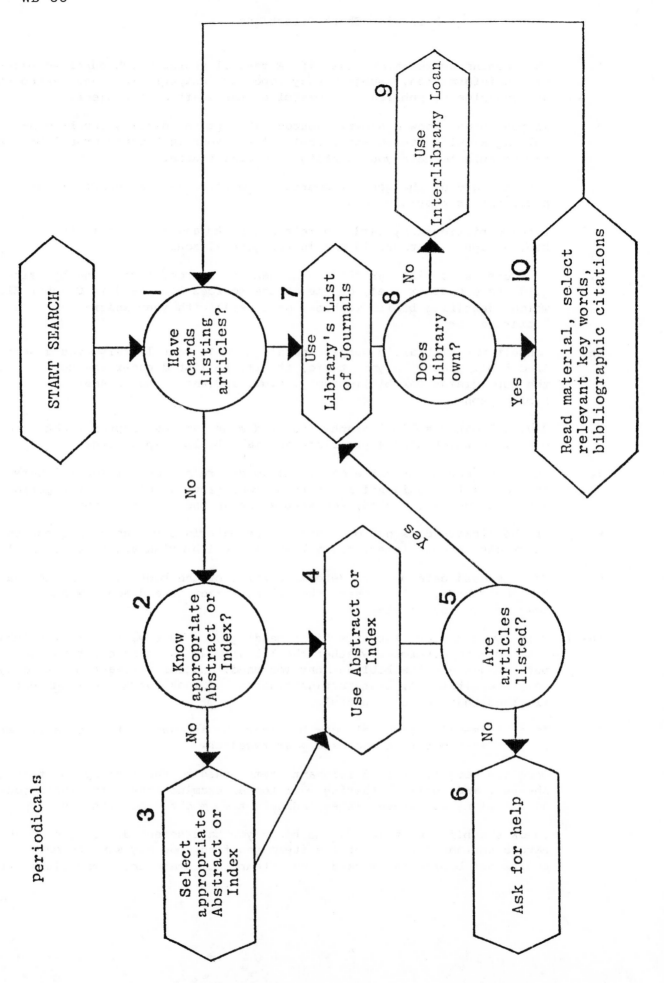

START SEARCH

1 Have cards listing articles?

No

7 Use Library's List of Journals

8 Does Library own?

No

9 Use Interlibrary Loan

Yes

10 Read material, select relevant key words, bibliographic citations

2 Know appropriate Abstract or Index?

No

3 Select appropriate Abstract or Index

4 Use Abstract or Index

5 Are articles listed?

Yes

No

6 Ask for help

Periodicals Flow Chart Directions

1. From your work to this point, you probably have
    bibliography cards for some periodical articles. To find
    out if the library owns the journals, go to step seven.
    To locate other articles which might be of use,

2. Consult appropriate abstracts and indexes (see Chapter
    Seven).

3. If you are not sure which abstracts or indexes would be
    useful, consult a guide (see Chapter One), a librarian or
    your instructor.

4. Using your master list of subject headings, consult the
    appropriate sections in the abstracts and indexes.

5. If useful articles are listed, copy complete citations
    and go to step seven. If not,

6. Ask a reference librarian for assistance, inasmuch as you
    may be using inappropriate subject headings. Not all
    indexes use the same terms for subject headings.

7-8. To determine whether the library owns the journals
    containing the articles you wish to consult, check the
    serials list or file which identifies the journals owned
    by the library.

9. If the library does not own the material, request it on
    interlibrary loan.

10. As you begin reading the articles you have selected,
    check the bibliographies. If you do not have citations
    for some of the items you find, you may want to make
    additional bibliography cards and attempt to locate these
    materials later.

It bears repeating that not all these steps will always
be necessary. In some cases, for example, articles may be the
only available sources of information. In other cases,
newspapers and government publications will be appropriate
sources and students should use the finding aids discussed in
Chapters 11 and 12. The steps outlined here are intended to
provide a wide overview of the information gathering process.

Emphasis has been placed on procedures for locating materials in the belief that once students have developed efficient and effective information locating techniques, they will save time that can be better spent in reading the appropriate sources they have found and in writing.

Chapter 13

RESEARCH PAPER MECHANICS AND METHODOLOGY

Assignment

Select a topic and prepare a bibliography as if you were going to write a 20-page research paper. The bibliography should be on three-by-five cards using the style suggested in this chapter. Along with the bibliography, turn in a three- to five-page typed "journal" or "log" of your research work. Write down each step you take as you take it, and explain why you decided to take that step. For example, when you consult a reference work, record its title, your reason for consulting it, and what, if any, use it was to you. Also, turn in your research record cards and subject headings list.

Each bibliography should include: basic sources for the topic; the major publications dealing with the topic; and publications dealing with the most recent developments. The research topic for the bibliography must be approved in advance.

APPENDIX

Chapter 1 - Guides to the Literature

Nunn, G. Raymond. Asia: A Selected and Annotated Guide to Reference Books. Cambridge, Mass.: M. I. T. Pr., 1971.

Horecky, Paul Louis, ed. East Central Europe: A Guide to Basic Publications. Chicago: University of Chicago Pr., 1969.

Fingerhut, Eugene R. The Fingerhut Guide: Sources in American History. Santa Barbara, Calif.: American Bibliographic Center--Clio Pr., 1973.

Bemis, Samuel F. and Grace G. Griffin. Guide to the Diplomatic History of the United States, 1775-1921. Washington, D. C.: Government Printing Office, 1935.

Paetow, Louis J. Guide to the Study of Medieval History. Rev. ed. prep. under the auspices of the Medieval Academy of America. New York: Kraus Reprint, 1931.

U. S. Library of Congress. General Reference and Bibliography Division. A Guide to the Study of the United States of America. Washington, D. C.: Government Printing Office, 1960.

Bengston, Hermann. Introduction to Ancient History. Berkeley: University of California Pr., 1970.

Griffin, Charles C., ed. Latin America: A Guide to the Historical Literature. Austin: University of Texas Pr., 1971.

Pearson, James D. Oriental and Asian Bibliography: An Introduction with Some Reference to Africa. New York: Shoe String, 1966.

Webb, Herschel. Research in Japanese Sources: A Guide. New York: Columbia University Pr., 1965.

Horecky, Paul. Russia and the Soviet Union: A Bibliographic Guide to Western-Language Publications. Chicago: University of Chicago Pr., 1965.

White, Carl M. and associates. Sources of Information in the Social Sciences: A Guide to the Literature. 2nd ed. Chicago: American Library Association, 1973.

Chapter 2 - Handbooks

America Votes: A Handbook of Contemporary American Election Statistics. New York: Macmillan, 1956-.

Williams, Neville. Chronology of the Expanding World, 1492-1762. New York: McKay, 1969.

Storey, Robin Lindsay, comp. Chronology of the Medieval World. New York: McKay, 1973.

Williams, Neville. Chronology of the Modern World: 1763 to the Present Time. New York: McKay, 1967.

Martin, Michael, Rheta and Gabriel H. Lovett. An Encyclopedia of Latin-American History. Rev. ed. by L. Robert Hughes. Indianapolis: Bobbs-Merrill, 1968.

Mead, Frank Spencer. Handbook of Denominations in the United States. 5th ed. Nashville: Abingdon Pr., 1970.

London. University. School of Oriental and African Studies. Handbook of Oriental History. London: University of London, 1963.

Haydn, Joseph and Benjamin Vincent. Haydn's Dictionary of Dates and Universal Information Relating to All Ages and Nations. 1910; Rpt. New York: Dover Publications, 1969.

Steinberg, Sigfrid H. Historical Tables: 58 B.C. - A.D. 1972. 9th ed. New York: St. Martin's Pr., 1973.

How Wisconsin Voted, 1848-1972. Madison, Wis.: Institute of Government Affairs, University of Wisconsin-Extension, 1974.

Florinsky, Michael, ed. McGraw-Hill Encyclopedia of Russia and the Soviet Union. New York: McGraw-Hill, 1961.

Johnson, Thomas Herbert. Oxford Companion to American History. New York: Oxford University Pr., 1966.

Steinberg, Sigfrid H. and I. H. Evans. Steinberg's Dictionary of British History. 2nd ed. New York: St. Martin's Pr., 1971.

Chapter 3 - Yearbooks and Almanacs

Africa South of the Sahara. London: Europa Publications, 1971-.

The Europa Yearbook. London: Europa Publications, 1959-. Ed. 1-.

The Middle East and North Africa. London: Europa Publications, 1953/54-.
    1948-. (20th ed., 1973/74).

United Nations. Yearbook of the United Nations. New York: United Nations,
    Department of Public Information, 1947-.

The Yearbook of World Affairs. Published under the auspices of the London
    Institute of World Affairs. London: Stevens, v. 1-, 1947-.

Chapter 4 - Atlases

American Heritage. The American Heritage Pictorial Atlas of United
    States History, by the editors of American Heritage. New York:
    American Heritage, 1966.

Adams, Arthur E., Ian M. Matley and William O. McCagg. An Atlas of
    Russian and East European History. New York: Praeger, 1967.

Chew, Allan F. An Atlas of Russian History: Eleven Centuries of Changing
    Borders. Rev. ed. New Haven: Yale University Pr., 1970.

Heyden, A. A. M. van der and Howard Hayes Scullard. Atlas of the
    Classical World. London: Nelson, 1959.

Meer, Frederick van der and Christine Mohrmann. Atlas of the Early
    Christian World. Tr. and ed. by Mary F. Hedlund and H. H. Rowley.
    Nelson, 1958.

Paullin, Charles Oscar. Atlas of the Historical Geography of the United
    States. Ed. by John K. Wright. Washington; New York: Carnegie
    Institute of Washington and the American Geographical Society, 1932.

Meer, Frederick van der. Atlas of Western Civilization. English version
    by T. A. Birrell. 2nd rev. ed. Princeton, N. J.: Van Nostrand, 1960.

Rand McNally and Co. Atlas of World History. Ed. by R. R. Palmer.
    Chicago: Rand McNally, 1965.

Herrmann, Albert. An Historical Atlas of China. New ed. Norton Ginsberg,
    Gen. ed. Chicago: Aldine, 1966.

Gaustad, Edwin Scott. Historical Atlas of Religion in America. New York:
    Harper, 1962.

U.S. Geological Survey. The National Atlas of the United States of America.
    Washington, D. C.: 1970.

Oxford Economic Atlas of the World. Prepared by the Cartographic Department
    of the Clarendon Press. London: Oxford University Pr., 1954-.

Rand McNally and Co. Rand McNally Commercial Atlas and Marketing Guide.
New York: Rand McNally, 1876-. Annual.

Gilbert, Martin. Recent History Atlas: 1870 to the Present Day.
Cartography by John R. Flower. New York: Macmillan, 1969.

Bartholomew (John) and Son Ltd. The Times Atlas of the World. Comprehensive Edition. [5th ed.] New York: Quadrangle/New York Times, 1975.

U. S. Military Academy (West Point). Department of Military Art and
Engineering. The West Point Atlas of American Wars. New York:
Praeger, 1959. 2 vols.

Chapter 5 - Subject Dictionaries and Encyclopedias

Plano, Jack C. and Milton Greenberg. The American Political Dictionary.
New York: Holt, Rinehart and Winston, 1967.

The Cambridge Ancient History. 3rd ed. London: Cambridge University Pr.,
1970-.

The Cambridge History of Africa. New York: Cambridge University Pr.,
1977-.

The Cambridge History of the British Empire. New York: Cambridge University
Pr., 1929-59.

The Cambridge Medieval History. Cambridge, Eng.: University Pr., 1964-67.

Dictionary of the History of Ideas: Studies of Selected Pivotal Ideas.
New York: Scribner, 1973.

Quick, John. Dictionary of Weapons and Military Terms. New York: McGraw-
Hill, 1973.

Encyclopaedia of the Social Sciences. New York: Macmillan, 1935.

Great Soviet Encyclopedia. New York: Macmillan, 1973.

Gebhart, Bruno. Handbuch der deutschen Geschichte. 8th ed. Stuttgart:
Union Verlag, 1954-59.

International Encyclopedia of the Social Sciences. New York: Macmillan,
1968. 17 vols.

The Modern Encyclopedia of Russian and Soviet History. Gulf Breeze, Fla.:
Academic International Pr., 1976-.

Chapter 6 - Biographical Dictionaries

Slocum, Robert B. Biographical Dictionaries and Related Works: An
    International Bibliography of Collective Biographies.... Detroit:
    Gale Research Co., 1967. 1st suppl. 1972.

Biographical Dictionaries Master Index: A Guide to More than 725,000
    Listings in More than Fifty Current Who's Who and Other Works of
    Collected Biography. Detroit: Gale Research Co., 1975-.

Boorman, Howard L. Biographical Dictionary of Republican China. New
    York: Columbia University Pr., 1967-71. 4 vols.

Wakelyn, Jon L. Biographical Dictionary of the Confederacy. Westport,
    Conn.: Greenwood Pr., 1977.

Chase, Harold et al. Biographical Dictionary of the Federal Judiciary.
    Detroit: Gale Research Co., 1976.

Biographical Directory of the American Congress, 1774-1971. Washington,
    D. C.: Government Printing Office, 1971.

Biographical Directory of the U. S. Executive Branch, 1774-1971. Westport,
    Conn.: Greenwood, 1971.

Congressional Directory. Washington, D. C.: Government Printing Office,
    1892-.

Hyamson, Albert M. A Dictionary of Universal Biography of All Ages and
    All Peoples. 2nd ed. London: Routledge and Kegan Paul Ltd., 1951.

Dictionnaire de biographie francaise. Paris: Letouzey et Ane, 1933-.

Neue deutsche Biographie. Berlin: Duncker & Humblot, 1953-.

Who's Who. London: A. & C. Black, Ltd., 1849-.

Who's Who in America: A Biographical Dictionary of Notable Living Men and
    Women. Chicago: A. N. Marquis Co., 1899-.

Who's Who in American Politics. Paul A. Theis and Edmund L. Henshaw, Jr.,
    eds. New York: Bowker, 1968.

Who's Who in Germany. Munich: Intercontinental Book & Pub. Co., 1956-.

Who's Who in Government. Chicago: Marquis, 1972-.

Who's Who in Latin America; A Biographical Dictionary of Notable Living
    Men and Women of Latin America. 3rd ed. Detroit, Mich.: Blaine
    Ethridge-Books, 1971.

Who's Who in History. New York: Barnes and Noble, 1966. 4 vols.

Who Was Who. London: A. & C. Black, Ltd., 1920-.

Who Was Who in America. Chicago: Marquis Who's Who, 1943.

Chapter 7 - Indexes and Abstracts

Absees: Soviet and East European Abstract Series, Glasgow Institute of
Soviet and East European Studies, University of Glasgow, 1970-.

Biography Index. New York: Wilson, vol. 1-, 1946/49-.

British Humanities Index. London: Library Association, 1962-.

Public Affairs Information Service. Bulletin. New York: 1915-.

Combined Retrospective Index to Journals in History, 1838-1974.
Washington, D. C.: Carrollton Pr., 1977.

Public Affairs Information Service. Foreign Language Index. New York:
1968-.

Poole's Index to Periodical Literature, 1802/81-1902/06. Gloucester,
Mass.: Peter Smith, 1963.

Readers' Guide to Periodical Literature. New York: Wilson, 1905-.

Social Sciences Index. New York: Wilson, 1974-.

Chapter 8 - Bibliographies

The American Bibliography of Russian and East European Studies. Columbus:
Ohio State University Pr., 1956-.

Conference on British Studies. Anglo-Norman England, 1066-1154. London:
Cambridge University Pr., 1969.

The Association of Asian Studies. Bibliography of Asian Studies. Ann
Arbor, Mich.: 1941-.

Davies, Godfrey. Bibliography of British History: Stuart Period, 1603-
1714. 2nd ed. Oxford: Clarendon Pr., 1970.

Pargellis, Stanley and D. J. Medley. Bibliography of British History:
The Eighteenth Century, 1714-1789. Oxford: Clarendon Pr., 1951.

Hersch, Gisela. A Bibliography of German Studies, 1945-1971. Bloomington,
Ind.: Indiana University Pr., 1972.

Gropp, A. E. A Bibliography of Latin American Bibliographies. Metuchen,
N. J.: Scarecrow, 1968. Suppl. 1971.

Trask, David F. A Bibliography of U. S.-Latin American Relations since 1810: A Selected List of 11,000 Published References. Lincoln: University of Nebraska Pr., 1968.

Foreign Affairs Bibliography. New York: Russell & Russell, 1960; New York: Bowker, 1964-.

British Museum. General Catalogue of Printed Books. London: Trustees of the British Museum, 1959-66. Supplements 1968-.

Handbook of Latin American Studies. Gainesville, Fla.: University of Florida Pr., no. 1-, 1935-.

International Bibliography of Historical Sources. Paris: International Committee of Historical Sciences, 1926-.

Horak, Stephan M. Junior Slavica: A Selected Annotated Bibliography of Books in English on Russia and Eastern Europe. Rochester, N. Y.: Libraries Unlimited, 1968.

The National Union Catalog of Manuscript Collections. Ann Arbor, Mich.: T. W. Edwards, 1962-.

Conference on British Studies. Restoration England, 1660-1689. Cambridge: University Pr., 1971.

American Universities Field Staff. A Select Bibliography: Asia, Africa, Eastern Europe, Latin America. New York: 1960.

British Museum. Subject Index, 1881-. London: 1902-.

Conference on British Studies. Victorian England, 1837-1901. Cambridge: University Pr., 1970.

Writings on American History. Washington, D. C.: American Historical Association, 1902-.

Royal Historical Society. Writings on British History, 1901-1933. New York: Barnes and Noble, 1968-70. 5 vols.

Chapter 9 - Scholarly Journals

Periodicals

American Historical Review. Washington, D. C.: American Historical Association, 1895-.

English Historical Review. London: Longmans, Green, 1886-.

Hispanic American Historical Review. Durham, N. C.: Duke University Pr., 1940-.

Isis: An International Review Devoted to the History of Science and Its
    Cultural Influences. Cambridge, Mass.: Harvard University Pr., 1913-.

Journal of African History. New York: Cambridge University Pr., 1960-.

Journal of American History. Bloomington, Ind.: Organization of American
    Historians, 1964-.

Journal of Contemporary History. London: Sage Publications, Ltd., 1966-.

Journal of Modern History. Chicago: University of Chicago Pr., 1929-.

Journal of Southern History. New Orleans, La.: Southern Historical
    Association, Tulane University, 1935-.

Pacific Historical Review. Berkeley, Calif.: University of California
    Pr., 1932-.

Slavic Review; American Quarterly of Soviet and East European Studies.
    Seattle, Wash.: American Assn. for the Advancement of Slavic Studies,
    University of Washington, 1901-.

Speculum; A Journal of Medieval Studies. Cambridge, Mass.: Medieval
    Academy of America, 1926-.

Wisconsin Magazine of History. Madison, Wis. State Historical Society
    of Wisconsin, 1917-.

Guides to Periodicals

Historical Periodicals; An Annotated World List of Historical and Related
    Serial Publications. Santa Barbara, Calif.: American Bibliographical
    Center--Clio Pr., 1961.

Ulrich's International Periodicals Directory. New York: Bowker, 1959/60-.

Chapter 10 - Evaluating Book-Length Studies

African Studies Association. ASA Review of Books. Waltham, Mass.: 1975-.

Modern Language Association of America. The MLA Style Sheet. 2nd ed.
    New York: 1971.

Reviews in European History: A Journal of Criticism--The Renaissance to the
    Present. Westport, Conn.: Redgrave Publishing Co., vol. 1-, 1974-75-.

Chapter 11 - Newspapers

American Newspapers 1821-1936. New York: Wilson, 1937.

U. S. Library of Congress. Union Catalog Division. Newspapers in Microform, 1948-1972. Washington, D. C.: 1973.

Palmer's Index to the Times Newspaper, 1790-June 1941. London: S. Palmer, 1868-1943.

Wall Street Journal Index. Princeton, N. J.: Dow Jones.

Washington Post Index. Worster, Ohio: Newspaper Indexing Center, Bell and Howell, 1972-.

Chapter 12 - Government Publications

U. S. Superintendent of Documents. Catalogue of the Public Documents of the...Congress...and of all Departments of the Government of the United States.... Washington, D. C.: Government Printing Office, 1896-1940.

CIS/Index to Publications of the United States Congress. Washington, D. C.: James B. Adler, 1970-.

CIS/US Serial Set Index, 1789-1969. Washington, D. C.: Congressional Information Service, 1977-.

Ames, John G. Comprehensive Index to the Publications of the United States Government 1881-1893. Washington, D. C.: Government Printing Office, 1905.

Kanely, Edna A. Cumulative Guide to U. S. Bibliographies, 1924-1973. Washington, D. C.: Carrollton Pr., 1976. 6 vols.

Poore, Ben. A Descriptive Catalog of the Government Publications of the United States, September 5, 1774-March 4, 1881. Washington, D. C.: Government Printing Office, 1885.

Schmeckebier, Lawrence F. and Roz B. Eastin. Government Publications and Their Use. 2nd rev. ed. Washington, D. C.: The Brookings Institution, 1969.

Index to Current Urban Documents. Westport, Conn.: Greenwood, 1972/73-.

U. S. Library of Congress. Popular Names of U. S. Government Reports. Washington, D. C.: Government Printing Office, 1976.

Chapter 13 - Research Paper Mechanics and Methodology

U. S. Library of Congress. Library of Congress Subject Headings. 8th ed. Washington, D. C.: 1975.

Modern Language Association of America. The MLA Style Sheet. 2nd ed. New York: 1971.